Repeat Offender

Also by Philip Bryer

<u>Fiction</u>
None of Your Business
On The Firm

<u>Non-fiction</u>
Why The Long Face? – The Paper Trail...

Repeat Offender

By

Philip Bryer

Based on an original invitation from Shane Kirk and Neale Foulger.

TOWNSEND PUBLISHING

This first edition by Townsend Publishing 2014

Copyright © Philip Bryer 2014

The moral right of the author has been asserted

All rights reserved

Without limiting the rights under copyright reserved above, no part of this publication may be reproduced, stored in or introduced into a retrieval system, or transmitted, in any form or by any means (electronic, mechanical, photocopying, recording or otherwise), without the prior written permission of the copyright owner

ISBN 978-0-9561544-3-9

Introduction

*S*ome years ago I was asked to become a regular contributor to the radio show Why The Long Face? In 2011 I put together the first book of the best of my weekly contributions, titled *Why The Long Face – The Paper Trail...*

Sadly, but in the spirit of if you keep moving then they can't hit you, the presenters chose to discontinue *Why The Long Face?* in radio form. However, its spirit lives on in this, the second collection of the best broadcasted bits. Not the rejects, not a second-rate sequel, but a Volume II of all new material. With pictures.

Philip Bryer

philipbryer@gmail.com

P.S. There will be regular mention in these pages of 'Sandra'. It is my barely deserved great good fortune that Sandra is my wife.

Foreword*

*Volume I of this series had 2 forewords. Bit of a long story, suffice to say a deal was finally brokered by the UN, ACAS and RAJAR.

In an attempt to even things up and perhaps recalibrate the Earth to the year 1975, this edition has no foreword.

Table of Contents

Hydra	11
Bolt	14
Copper	17
Effect	20
Poncateria	23
Con	25
Changes	28
Aid	31
Bugs	34
Vino	37
Joannas	41
Hamburg	44
Questions	47
Whodunit	51
Outing	54
Shop	57
Akip	59
Fugitive	62
Lodger	65
Last	67
Say	70
Old	72
Devil	74
Popping	77
Turn	80

Spiders	82
Orders	85
Jokerman	87
Fizz	90
Hat	92
Liar	95
Badge	97
Snip	100
Fight	103
Happy	106
High	109
Sick	111
Shortcut	114
Stewart	117
Titfer	119
Snapper	122
Bob	125
Heaven	127
Safe	130
Hobby	132
Formality	134
Fete	137
Birds	140
Musical	143
Film	145

Hydra

Invincible. Full Power. Extreme. Invisible. Indestructible. Bulldog.

What do all of those describe, then? Aircraft carriers? Spaceships? Jet fighters?

Power Wash. Root Power Restorative. Defence. M-Lotion. Age Resolve.

Well, to give you a clue, the full name of one of them is *Invincible Extreme Protection* and *Indestructible* refers to a hair gel. Yes, it's time to cross the border into the rather peculiar land that is men's toiletries. A reassuringly macho spot where a shampoo directed at tackling thinning hair makes no mention of baldness, but is called, hey big boy, *Body Building*. A place where we are directed to observe the 5 signs of male skin fatigue. 'Listen guys, I'm tired and so is my skin.' Female skin fatigue must be a whole different bunch of dermatitis.

Try this moisturiser fellahs, it's *Hydra Energetic*. What the ...? I looked up *Hydra*. It's either a serpent-like monster from Greek Mythology, or a Greek island, or a simple fresh-water animal possessing radial symmetry, or to stretch belief rather too far, in the final case The Hydra is a terrorist organisation given to us by comic outfit, Marvel.

Oddly, in the ads themselves, all of the blokes with skin conditions, BO and dandruff look so bloody pleased with themselves – all wearing the default expression of Robbie Williams.

Max Advance. Multi Action. Max Comfort. Max Instant.

In this company, something called *Post Shave Healer* sounds positively fey. Positively Fey, currently on tour of course with Florence and the Machine. In session tonight and there'll be three more from them later.

Someone I know got heavily into the male grooming thing. I mean, fair do's, he was perhaps driven into soapy submission by a succession of Christmas gift packs. He took to employing a swipe of pre-shave balm, a moisturising finish, and a dab of afters. Taking things further, scrubbing and exfoliation took place, hair was gelled up or waxed for weekend nights out, and when in a particularly fussy mood, a little plucking would take place, and loose, perceived to be out-of-place, hair would be tweezered away.

One night, two weeks before the wedding, his fiancée spoke to him.

'I'm worried," she said, "that you might be turning into a girl.'

Years ago and after my first few months of commuting into London, pounding the streets and the underground, the doctor advised me that the eczema I was suffering was due to stress. So I had this shampoo, and that conditioner, and a lotion and a rub and, you know what my eczema-free old man used to wash his hair in? Washing up liquid.

Welcome to the best of *Why The Long Face?* Pour homme et pour femme.

Bolt

*T*he handle fell off the side door to our garage a few years ago. There was a bit that was left poking out, some kind of spindle with holes in it. I simply jammed a six-inch nail through the hole nearest the door and *voilà*, I presented to the astonished audience of one who is known as Sandra, a brand new, improvised door handle.

"It's a complete one-off," I said.

She looked at me, her expression way over on the rank disbelief side of doubtful. *I* could live with it though. It never really occurred to me to invest the time in fixing it up with a shop-bought handle. 'Why have you got a nail for a door handle?' asked 5-year-old Lily.

"It's a complete one-off," I explained. "I bet none of your friends have got one like that."
The look on her face confirmed as much.

Sandra's requests that I fix it became less frequent, as she learned to live with it too.
"It works doesn't it?" I'd say, right up until the point that we had the builders in and one of them said he'd a got a doorknob on the van that would fit, and within moments and before I could protest we had a dreary old doorknob just like everyone else. I'll tell you something, with a Bryer-design-and-build-nail-knob you could open the door with a mere flick of your little finger even while laden down with a case of beer or a basket full of washing, and nobody can do that now that we have an inferior product that requires the grip and attention of the whole hand.

We have a gate at the side of the house which has never shut properly because the bolt and the thing the bolt is supposed to slide into are slightly on the piss. The bolt sits in at an angle and so the merest zephyr of wind which causes the slightest sway to the gate means the bolt pops out way too readily. Not too much of a problem, although a bit of a nuisance when the latch broke. On particularly windy nights I've been known to bung a breezeblock behind the gate to stop it swinging open. Job done. Yesterday someone fitted a new latch and, unbidden, produced bits of wood and big, flat saw with knobs and levers that looked like some sort of torture device. I gave him no more than a quizzical look. 'All will be revealed,' he said, and that's good enough for me. Please don't go into long, technical explanations of why A doesn't work and how it's going to fit together perfectly with B once you've performed Job C. I'll make you a cup of tea and disappear and you can give me a shout when you've finished.

The thing is, it wouldn't occur to me to cut a piece of wood at an angle and fix it to the…Ah, I'm doing the very thing I just said I didn't want to happen. However, so pleased was I with the result that I spent a few minutes standing at the gate playing with the new fitting and repeating, "Bolt slides in, bolt slides out." Awesome.

This is a house where the *10% off this weekend at Homebase* leaflets go straight into the bottom recesses of the recycling box before anyone else gets a chance to see them. The sales assistant in Smiths handed me a B&Q voucher recently and I took great pleasure in politely handing it back.

I bought a piece of gardening equipment online recently that I could have easily got in the DIY hangar down the road, but the £6.95 delivery charge seemed a fair price to pay for not actually having to go there.

A good Aussie friend of mine, Adam, recently bought a big old place in Melbourne. He works hard, earns very well, and has a wife and two young kids. 'Any tips on the decorating?' he asked me over Skype one Sunday morning.

"Yes," I replied firmly, "pay someone else to do it."

Copper

Evenin' all. Perhaps I should explain for younger readers that *Evenin' all* was how TV copper Sergeant George Dixon opened every episode of ancient police drama show *Dixon of Dock Green*. Quite an achievement considering that his character got bumped off by teenage hoodlum Dirk Bogarde in the film *The Blue Lamp* some years before. Anyway, it's clear that there was an early Saturday evening audience for a gentle drama featuring a use-your-common-sense, stay-on-the-straight-and-*narrer*, clip-em-round-the-ear sort of wise old copper.

The sort of copper who walked the beat. Perhaps I should explain, again for younger readers, that the old bill haven't always got around by helicopter, or in cars with siren set permanently to the ON position and which only drop below 90 miles-an-hour when they hit someone. They used to sort of leave the police station on foot and walk about all day. The, um, laughably outdated theory being that their frequent and visible presence on the streets would deter the wrongdoer from doing wrong deeds. Hmmm.

On the occasions when the fuzz needed to get around a bit more sharpish, perhaps to nab some villains who'd had it away on their toes, they jumped in something called a panda car.

Younger readers....you'll just have to trust me on this, back then, in a move no doubt designed to strike fear and trepidatious career-changing choices in felons far and wide, the chariots of law enforcement really were named after the cutest animals on the planet.

How we have moved on.

'There's a police car outside,' said Sandra.

Tap, tap, tap on the door. Which I open. There is indeed a police car, and in front of me, a plain-clothes upholder of the law and servant of the public. I assume.

'Mr Lloyd?' he asked, in not entirely pleasant fashion.
"No," I replied, simply.
'You're not Mr Lloyd?'
"No I'm not," I shrugged.

He consulted his clipboard.

'Is Steven Lloyd in?'

He didn't seem to be catching the drift.

"No, nobody called Lloyd lives here and by the way, *who are you?*"
'Oh,' he fished in his pocket and pulled out his ID. I forget the name, but doubtless it was Detective Sergeant Superbrain or some-such. 'It's about the *car*,' he said, as if addressing a three-year-old.

"Which car would that be?"

'The car that got smashed up'.

I took a breath.

"Look," I said, "I have no idea what you're talking about."

'Right, you've never heard of Mr Lloyd and he doesn't live here and you don't know anything about a smashed up car?'

"Correct," I said.

'And I suppose this isn't number 43 either?'

The thing is, I find that if you're going to lace your statements with sarcasm and be all accusatory and smart-arse, well, you'd best get your facts right. I said nothing. Eventually he looked up from his clipboard, a rather superior smile played about his lips. For a moment. Until he saw me pointing up at the big, black iron numbers which stood out really well against the fresh white paint of our front door. A **5** and an **8**. I smiled back.

He scuttled off. No apology, nothing. Funny thing is, this conversation was replayed almost in full about a year later with another local Clouseau.

Wouldn't have happened in Sergeant George Dixon's day. I might have got fitted up, but, thanks to years of pounding the beat at least he'd have known who lived where.

Effect

'*H*ave you taken these before?'
"Yeah, yeah, yeah."
'Are you taking anything else?'
"No, no, no."

(Thinks: just hand 'em over. It's only Solpadeine or Benylin or Nytol).

Generally, I always thought that the side effects of medication were rather overstated. I held this truth to be self-evident until Sandra I went on holiday to an exotic location which was set slap bang in the Indian Ocean and offered malaria as an extra option but one in which the unwary had no choice. So we geared up with the one-a-day catch-all pill, Larium. No problem, for me at least. However, for the lovely Mrs Bryer, problem. She started to suffer terrible nausea round about evening meal times. Most memorably round about the time that our market-price special occasion dinner arrived. A waiter hauled this table-top-sized platter from the kitchen, struggling under the weight of a dozen jumbo prawns as big as lobsters and topped with a couple of lobsters, each the size of the average toddler, and all arranged on a bed of crispy rainforest.

"Are you OK?" I asked the wraith with the grey pallor who sat opposite, having somehow replaced the gorgeous vision of womanhood with whom I'd just shared a cocktail.
'Got to go back to the room, feel terrible.'

I looked at the spread, the fresh seafood, the salad, the booze in the ice-bucket. I made a move to get up, "Well, if you're not well…"

'You stay and have dinner, I'm OK,' she said, 'it's just the pills.'
"Well," I replied, "If you're sure.."

No sense in wasting it, we'd all have done the same, just a passing sickness, it's what she would have wanted.

'How was dinner?' asked Sandra.
"Alright," I replied, carefully.
'Did you save me any?'
"I think what you need to do," I said confidently, "is take the pills when we go to bed at night and that way it won't spoil your mealtimes."
'You didn't save me any did you?'

Once, rammed full of morphine and anaesthetic, I spent all night wide-awake after surgery, writing and rehearsing my ward round case for not being kept in hospital for an additional 3 days, as I'd been tipped off I might be. But when the man came round and said I was free to go I was on such a high that I phoned the office at 8:30 AM and announced rather grandly that I would be returning to work in the morning. Which is the first time that I'd held a business-related conversation while smacked off my tits. Thankfully my boss is a reasonable man and when he sussed the chemically-induced reasons for my call and forbade my return for at least a week I was happy to oblige. And the flashing rainbows in my peripheral vision that I experienced for the next week confirmed by belief in 2 things: 1. He was right and 2. I should ease up on the Tramadol. Particularly when things began to get a lot more blurry.

My mother's just out of intensive care after a post-surgery, close as *Knockin' on Heaven's Door* brush with mortality. They took her off morphine soon enough. As she said, with some, perhaps wistful, relief, 'I've been on all these trips'.

Poncateria

Whether official or unofficial, most workplaces have their approved social gathering places. A Pub, a restaurant, and as shown in *Life On Mars* on their visit to that direst of decades, in the Eighties stupid blokes (including me) really did affect the skinny tie and jacked up the sleeves of their jackets, and girls puffed up their shoulder pads and fluffed out their barnets to the outer limits, and all to go to deeply silly and pretentious places called wine bars.

Then there are approved zones within approved places. When I worked for a London magazine publisher, The Stamford Arms was *the* place to go. However, it wasn't quite that simple, because our department's area was always, but always, *Upstairs at the Stammie*. In a particular corner area by the bar. Not in the opposite corner, or, if we were ever usurped by early-comers (which wasn't often) at one of the far ends so distant from our box seats that it made us very disconcerted and also rather jealous, but at least it wasn't downstairs, which was particular no-no. Downstairs was nowhere near as bespoke and exclusive as upstairs, populated as it was by people so unaware that they probably had no idea there even *was* an upstairs.

There have been rumblings at the current workplace because the place with company accreditation and which was included in my employer's discount card scheme has been tweaking their special offers. No more free soft drinks. No more free tea and coffee. But now that I hear that some tightwads and moochers were going in the purely for something off the free list, well, I can't say I blame the place one jot. But you should have heard the bleating from the mooching contingent. Oh, how dare they deprive people who, after all, are on a reasonably good screw, of the chance to take up valuable lunchtime space and all that goes with it, just to save themselves a pound.

Although it's not my idea of a lunchtime hotspot. For it's not so much the sophisticated brasserie it likes to think it is, but more of a licensed works canteen. Table service too. Table service? You're a boozer (and not a very good one). Get over it.

I don't like table service when I'm out for a beer and a sandwich. I feel deeply uncomfortable with the notion of sitting down at a table and someone bringing me a pint. I like to take delivery of a pint of bitter while standing at the bar so I can take off the top inch or two, have a look round and ponder my next move. Then, and only then, might I take them up on their offer of seating. Generally though, I'd rather assume man's natural position at the bar with one foot resting on the brass rail and, well, I'm not sure what to do with the other foot now, since it's no longer desirable, or indeed legal, to use it to stub one's fags out.

Basically, I'm suspicious of an official company haunt. If they want me in there, then that's a blindingly good reason for going somewhere else. I get the feeling I'm being watched. That my office door entry fob is somehow registering the fact that I've had 3 pints and have been in there for an hour-and-a-half with no sign yet of coming up for air. So, free this-and-that or 2-for-1's or whatnot, I care not. Not feeling the need to compromise my independence for a free drink in a *poncateria* I returned my reward card in protest at Britain's involvement in the Iraq War and my illustrated *Why The Long Face...The Paper Trail* book slipping down the Amazon charts.

Con

*J*ust threw out a Calvin Klein shirt. Well, when I say *Calvin Klein* I'd better clarify, I'm not normally one for designer gear. Levi's being about the only brand I specify, and as they're not as comfortable as they once were I might have to move onto Farahs or those 3-for-twenty-quid jobs you see in the colour supplements. You know, with the elasticated waistband.

Also, when I say a *Calvin Klein shirt*, understand that I bought 3 for a tenner in Bangkok 10 years ago and this one has finally split down the side and started shedding buttons. Three for a tenner and lasted ten years – bargain, certainly not a con.

Unlike the time I bought a local paper from a bloke on the main square in Antigua, retired to a bar while Sandra went shopping, ordered a cold beer and settled down to read the local news, only to discover that the crafty bastard had sold me yesterday's. In hindsight, he wasn't sitting by a stack of papers as you might expect, but rather he only appeared to have one copy which he offloaded to me for a dollar before scurrying off. Nice work.

I admired that one. Unlike the familiar sight of the taxi driver who has a bottles of, ahem, Chanel No.5 arrayed along his dashboard, which he's selling because, oh, because they're fire-damaged, or his mate gets a discount because he works there – oh, at that famous Chanel No.5 factory in Brentford, you mean? Beware cabbies bearing fake scents. In addition, beware Singapore market traders. Particularly those who are knocking out CDs.

I bought 2 Beatles compilations and an Eagles one in Singapore. It wasn't until we got back to our friends' place and put one of them on that the realisation hit me like a wet fish straight in the chops. This is less *The Beatles* and more like the worst covers band you ever heard. This sounds like me and my mates did back then when we were trying to sound like

T Rex, only they lack our instinctive feel and the presence of 3 bongo players in a band of 4. A glance at the track listings confirms it: *Norwegian Woody, Eight Weeks of a Day, And Your Boy Can Sing,* and the unforgettable, *It's Been Hard Days Head.* Still, it was a laugh, and the version of *Yellow Submarine* which sounds like it was done in my shed on a cassette recorder is a thing of shock, awe and unintentional hilarity.

Then there was the time in Kenya, walking along the seafront when a lanky old geezer in tribal robes stopped and bowed and asked me very politely if I would mind sending him some stamps from England. He offered a scrap of paper with his address on. *Well, why not?* I thought, *be a nice thing to do for the old chap.* "OK," I said. Well, then he said, come and meet the family. Sandra and I exchanged a look, *Well, why not? Be a nice thing to do.* Slice of real life and all that.

It wasn't far. When we arrive, he goes off and reappears with some 'family' members and they proceed to give Sandra a handbag and some 'silver' bangles. We protest, far too generous, cannot possibly accept, let me pay you something.. If you insist, says the old boy, some bait for my fishing for when I go out on my *dhow.* I walk this way, through a very narrow entrance to a dark and dingy shed which is full of ugly bastard types bearing the traditional attire of scars and tattoos which they accessorised most inventively with a large serving of threatening behaviour. A handful of fish guts and heads in a clear plastic bag are produced from a freezer, for which they sting me £25. Which is quite fair when you think about it. At least it is as an alternative to playing the central role in the *There's Still No Sign Of The British Man Who Went Missing In Kenya Three Weeks Ago* story on News at Ten.

Changes

*T*here are things that I don't do anymore.

I don't drink whisky. I stopped drinking whisky a long time ago, and, while I didn't drink a lot of it, I stopped because it made me feel ill.

I don't go to bed after midnight on a work night. Years ago I used to go out on a Thursday and invariably stay up all night, pausing only to go home for a shower and a change of clothes at 6-ish before heading off to work.

I don't have to turn on some form of music as soon as I enter a room. Not always, anyway. This changed after I spent a couple of weeks in hospital a few years ago, and I have no idea why.

I don't wait for hours after having a meal before I feel it's safe enough to go swimming without getting cramp and sinking.

If I burn myself I don't slap a knob of butter on the searing flesh.

Thanks to my mother I believed the last two for years.

I don't possess a pair of trainers, not particularly for aesthetic reasons, I just feel that there's a time when men should stop wearing them, but strangely, in the past couple of years I have developed a bit of a girly footwear fetish and still get a buzz from pulling on my Kurt Geiger slip-ons with the fake lace-holes.

Time was on a Saturday I would rise with hangover, and my housemate Dave and I would breakfast on fatty fried things and watch *Gazzetta Football Italia, Football Focus* with 'Boring' Bob Wilson, followed by *The Saint and Greavesie* on ITV before heading back to the boozer for another load. This morning, I had some muesli with soya milk and entered a competition to win a £1000 worth of gardening vouchers. And you know what? These days are better, plus I don't have a headache.

As night follows day, Sunday follows Saturday, and it's hard to explain what dreary old Sundays used to be like. There wasn't any sport to speak of. Football and rugby were done-and-dubbined for the week by a quarter-to-five on the Saturday. As for the so-called summer sports, well, Test Match cricket and Wimbledon tennis decided to limit the access the proletariat had to their rather exclusive offerings by shutting down on Sundays for a rest.

The only place to shop on a Sunday was the newsagent who opened briefly in the morning to enable you to get a Sunday paper, and tears, trial and tedium lurked menacingly in the post-lunch gloom for those who had nothing to read, for all Sunday afternoon radio had to offer was *Sing Something Simple* – Google it if you like, I can't bear to.

At least there was the pub, eh? Except, as those of us of a certain age remember, the pubs opened from noon until 2, and then, to bring them in line with the rest of the country's 'attractions', they shut down for the afternoon. Leaving a certain group of the populace spending the afternoon listening to Man LPs and waiting for the ceremonial drawing back of the bolts on the doors of the local at 7 o'clock.

7 o'clock! To sum up how much things have properly changed, at 7 o'clock on a Sunday night these days all I'm thinking about is going to bed.

Aid

*I*t occurs to me every now and then that I'd be useless in a crisis. I mean the sort of crisis which calls for someone to step forward from the crowd, approach the poor twisted wreckage of a human frame on the floor and say, "Stand back everyone, I'm a qualified first-aider".

Obviously I know it's bad form these days to apply butter to burned skin – er, like our mums' did, and you don't go tying off extremities with vice-tight tourniquets for you might just cause said extremity to drop off. Apply pressure to cuts and make sure the area spouting all of the claret is in a more elevated position than the heart – for a nasty cut on the foot, well, I'm not too sure but this may involve standing the patient on their head. I would have to address this potentially sticky issue nearer the time.

I think I could make a fair shake of the recovery position and the Heimlich, and I do know that if you see someone sinking to the bottom of a swimming pool with cramp it's bound to have been caused by them having a meal in the previous few hours and you're well within your rights to shout "I told you so," at their disappearing form as it gasps for a final breath.

Before I continue, I would like to stress that there is nothing funny about epilepsy. This story is about the *reaction* of people to a most unfortunate fellow and his epileptic seizure.

At the time I worked in an office with a couple of Kiwis, Mike who was a copper back in Auckland and Matthew who was, well, Matthew was a bit dim, bless him. He showed me a film once of a perpetual motion machine in which he had invested cash following receipt of an irresistible email. A bit dim, see? We took on a temp, Chris, who suffered with epilepsy. His last episode had been a year or so back and we found out later that he had taken it upon himself to stop taking his medication in the hope of getting his driving licence back.

This turned out to be a mistake.

It happened when Mike, the one person who would have known what to do, was back home on holiday. Credit to Matthew, because he had apparently asked Mike what to do in the event of Chris having an event, and Mike had said to keep the airway clear. One day, soon after lunch I heard a groan and looked up to see Chris, features locked in pained grimace, pitching sideways off his seat and hitting the deck hard. "I'll go and get the nurse," I yelled, my natural reaction to crisis being to run off and find someone else to deal with it. The medical centre was only a couple of floors away and the nurse and I ran back together.

'This man is bleeding,' said the nurse, 'has he bitten himself?'
'I don't know,' Matthew replied, and appropriately for a New Zealander, a little sheepishly.
'You might, er,' Matthew continued, 'you might find some bits of my pen in his mouth.'
'Pen? How did he get bits of pen in his mouth?'
'I put it there,' said Matthew.
'Why did you put a pen in his mouth?'
'Mike told me to,' said Matthew miserably.
'And where is this Mike?' asked the nurse.
'Oh, he's on holiday in New Zealand.'

Chris made a full recovery. Mike and I are still in touch, he moved to Christchurch and proved to be a handy bloke to have around in an earthquake, and, when last heard of, Matthew had invested heavily in the Nigerian lottery.

Bugs

*T*here's a lot of water around where we live, so at any time of year it seems that flying bugs and mosquitoes are queuing up at the kitchen door, banging a hopeful tattoo back and forth on the windows, seeking warmth and a safe passage to one of our veins. Where once in this country we had nothing more bothersome than gnats which were only seen for a steamy summer month or two, now there are big, mean, brother-sucking mozzies that are immune to frost and ice, and indeed it seems that the only effect of sub-zero temperatures is to stiffen their determination to bust their way in to the house.

Sometimes though, there are bigger beasts about.

We hadn't been living here long, and were still getting the place organised. It was early summer and we'd put some of the Kew Gardens-like collection of houseplants outside for a good douse and dust-off before bringing them back in. Sandra phoned me one afternoon at work.

"The-e-e-re-s, there's a.. ," she began.
"A what?" I replied impatiently, about to get all drama-queen-busy.
"S-s-ssssnake."
"Where?"
"In the kitchen."

It appears that Brer Snake had set up home outside in a trough which was full of plants and ferns and ivy which we'd recently brought back in from the garden. He'd been happily chomping his way through the insect life therein, and I guessed that once the food had run out he'd been forced to take a look round outside. Except he wasn't outside anymore, was he? And as he couldn't open the fridge he was reduced to scooting around the kitchen floor.

Until Mrs Bryer appeared and they spooked each other so much that Slippery Sid slid behind the cooker and Sandra built a barricade at the kitchen door which was reminiscent of the Hoover Dam.

As soon as I got in, I switched on the oven, all 4 cooker rings and the grill. "That'll force him out," I said confidently. Nothing. Sandra was good enough to remain, reasonably, silent, as I went into the *not with 3 barrels on him* routine from Jaws. So we secured the kitchen as best we could and left him to it. I walked in there at about 11, and there he sat, coiled up in the middle of the floor, hooded and about to strike – well, to be honest I'm not sure now about that last bit – anyway I bagged him up and gave him his freedom.

〰️

"At the end of the garden," I said.
'He'll just come back in,' said Sandra.
"For what? He knows there's nothing to eat. Unlike that lizard."

We'd sit on a wooden balcony outside our hotel room in Antigua. Having a gin, checking out the sea. A tiny lizard, size of my little finger, would sometimes join us. His head popping out from between the planks, he'd scout around for bugs, crumbs or grains of sugar. One evening, finding nothing, he got a little more ambitious. His tiny jaws soon found something to latch onto. My bloody big toe. By which the tenacious little fellow attempted to drag me through the decking to his lair. I just about emerged with a narrow victory on points.

When I was a kid my mates and I used to keep frogs, toads and slow worms that we'd found. Used to keep them in a big old tin bath that we filled with earth and stones and a little water. But often they'd expire through lack of food. One day, my best friend's dad, Mr Jones, showed us how to attract flies to our little zoo by dumping a richly odorous lump of poo in there. It was only later on that I realised where he must have sourced fresh ordure at such short notice. So he was either a great dad or a filthy old git. I still haven't quite decided.

Vino

"*A* bottle of the Liebfraumilch, please."

Because back then, nothing said *sophisticated man about town* quite as much as a bottle of cheap, overly sweet, sickly, mass-produced cats' piss. But if one really wanted to impress, then Blue Nun was the only way to go, and to take things a notch further then a bottle of Black Tower, in its imposing, black, er, tower of a bottle was guaranteed to reward. I mean they were both still too sweet and sickly, but a little less so, and they had the kudos of being a bit more expensive, and, believe me, this was important to a particular date who quaffed sweet Martini and lemonade as if from the bucket of a JCB. Every time her arm went up her mouth opened. But this is where we found ourselves. The dry Martini and lemonade girls were, at this early stage, playing a couple of leagues higher and remained tantalisingly out of reach. So it was a bottle of Liebfraumilch. Or Black Tower on payday.

It's been mentioned around the house that one day we might go to South Africa and do the wine trail. Sandra floated the idea before we went to California. You can go to the Napa Valley and, it turns out, pay a large amount of money for access to the vineyards, where they'll slip you the odd smear of barrel scrapings in one of those tiny plastic cups you get your pills in in hospital, and then charge you extra for a meagre spot of lunch. I know this because I asked someone who'd done it, and they warned me off. So when Sandra floated the idea, I made sure I torpedoed it without ado or hesitation.

Besides, it seems to me that the worst part of 'doing the wine trail' is not being stung by the winemakers, it's trawling around these places with a load of, well, I can do no better than James May's memorable description of the breed, a load of wine ponces. I'd be trapped in a nightmarish, twisting vortex of pretentiousness, of vanilla notes and hints of cherry and easy on the nose, and still no-one can tell me how grapes end up tasting like lemons or leather or freshly-mown grass.

Sucking through their teeth like they've had their jawbones kicked in and wired shut (oh, I wish), swirling and swooshing like dental patients, and then spitting like oikish footballers. Ugh. At least do the winemaker the honour of knocking it back. Reminds me of a *Private Eye* cartoon in which the waiter is showing the diner a bottle of wine and saying, 'May I recommend this one sir? I guarantee it'll get you pissed'.

I used to work for a magazine publisher, and we got wind one Friday afternoon of a wine tasting in one of the conference rooms. Firms would often come in offering freebies in the hope of press coverage. My friend James and I headed for the 7th Floor and steamed right in.
However, we were divested of our hastily-poured glasses and escorted back to the entrance – while being advised of the vital importance of starting at point A and moving on around the room and knocking back the turps in the proper sequence. We were also asked to sign in. 'Which magazine are you from?' asked the Head Wino. James spoke, 'Er, we're from admin,' "Yes, I continued, "Admin Magazine. It's quite a new venture, so if you wouldn't mind keeping it to yourself...?" I looked at the Head Wino meaningfully. 'Of course, sir, you can rely on me. Now, to start we've got a delicious, light, sauvignon blanc...' 'Have you got any nuts?' asked James. 'Er, no sir'. 'Or any food at all?' James continued, 'I don't really like wine'.

James didn't do so bad though. He even took the Head Man's business card with a straight face as we sampled the treacly reds at the finish. "£60 a bottle eh? 10% off for a case? Well, we'll certainly have a think about it, won't we James?"

And we did. We thought about it right up until we went next door to The Stamford Arms and ordered 2 pints of Directors.

Joannas

*W*e took in a number of musical delights on a trip to Las Vegas. The divine Gladys Knight, Cirque de Soleil's head-fudging Beatles show *Love*, and the hugely entertaining old rascal Rod Stewart. This is the tale of another musical evening.

"That looks like fun," we agreed, *The Duelling Pianos Show* in the Italian-styled Saluté Lounge at our hotel. And in we go, to a bar just off the casino floor, with 2 'grand pianos' set at an angle to each other, and a rotating cast of players. Fairly early on we twig that they're not actually grand pianos, but electric keyboards through which the talent can key in rhythm tracks as required. The better of the rotating cast can also play piano with one hand while using an iPad with the other to summon up details on requested tunes. For the audience in this bar, which was the size of a larger branch of Lush or Thornton's, are supplied with request forms and encouraged to wander up to the stage and deposit forms and cash into the glass bowls on each piano.

After we'd heard *Piano Man*, Anything by Elton John, and two songs by Journey. That's two songs by Journey just when you, the disbelieving public, thought satire was dead. *Two songs* by rotten old Journey, so I went up with dollars and my form, and this is what happened to my 3 choices:

High School Confidential by Jerry Lee Lewis
'Sorry, we don't know that one, but thanks for not requesting the usual ones we get asked to do.'
Nut Rocker by B Bumble and The Stingers
'Don't know that one either. But I think it's a remake.'

Waterloo Sunset

'Don't know that one, but I think it's from the 1972 album.'

"I think you'll find," I said to Sandra by way of gritted teeth, "*I think you'll find* that *Waterloo Sunset* came out in 1967, *actually*. Oh, well, he's having a go at *Lola*. OK." Then one of them played Air on a Bee Sting or something, (ahem, I'd suggest because *Nut Rocker* was, to be technical for a moment, too hard).

There's a Good Ole Boy at the front who whoops and hollers when he gets a Creedence or Johnny Cash track played (hardly known for the piano lounge sound, either of them, I'd say) and then he looks round to see who's joining with his handclaps and sing-alongs – scans the entire group. They start playing *American Pie*. And they pause after a couple of minutes and say, 'This is a long song, who wants us to stop now?" I raise my hand, and the withering riposte comes winging over from the stage. 'This is Vegas sir, not a schoolroom.' So I yelled back, "Stop now." After all 8 minutes of any music is too long for me nowadays unless it's Mozart.

'OK,' said Ivory Tinkler #1, 'Tell you what, if y'all sing the chorus real loud and clap your hands we'll do another verse.'

You know, I love America and American people, but Sandra and I sat on our hands, then the assembled crowd took the bloody roof off and we were treated to another verse before they put a sensible lid on it and played Piano

Man again and I didn't get shot, probably as a result of shrinking down in my seat.

We were just about to go, when from the stage I heard, 'You shake my nerves and you rattle my brain, too much love drives a man insane,' and were invited to sing along to Jerry Lee's *Great Balls of Fire*.

Sorry, but I don't know that one.

Hamburg

*O*ne of the most valuable things I've learned from my stays in hospital is that the night staff are far more obliging with the drugs, much more free and easy with the opiates than the day staff. How do I know this? Because the day staff told me, that's how.

Another handy tip, although this one is for visitors, even if your friend or relative's table is covered to bursting with stuff and you need to free up some room, those under-the-bedclothes urine caddies are not likely to balance on a radiator for long, however hard you stare at them. They are unlikely to survive the hour undisturbed or un-tipped. And should this happen during the coldest winter in almost 14 years when the thermostats throughout the building were set to *She cannae take any more, Captain*, just be aware that the aroma of seared urine is unlikely to assist in the healing process. Actually it reminded me of the soup the hospital kitchen had served up just the previous day.

Someone I know had a major operation and ended up with a chain of staples holding them together from throat to belly. As we all appreciate, everyone has to learn, and the best place to learn is on the job, so he cheerfully assented to a student nurse being entrusted with the task of carrying out their removal. However, so tricky was the procedure, so timorous the student that my friend ended up taking most of them out himself, with the remainder being pulled out in a joint effort. Rather like that Polar explorer who removed his own appendix with the aid of a mirror. As someone said at the time, 'I wouldn't have thought a mirror would be sharp enough'.

For what you need to survive in hospital, in addition to fistfuls of drugs, is a sense of humour.

Sandra's dad, Rex, had more than his share of health problems towards the end of his life, and on one occasion regaled us with tales of the morning's events as we sat at his Sussex hospital bedside.

'I had a blanket bath this morning,' he said, 'two lovely nurses they were. I said to them, 'you know I haven't had a time like this since I was in a knocking shop in Hamburg in 1945?''
"What did they say?" we asked.
'Oh, bugger all,' he replied, his voice gathering in volume, 'that's the trouble with these Sussex people, they've got no sense of humour, you see?'

I sensed there'd be no more blanket baths.

Out of hospital, Rex was suffering neck and shoulder pain. 'I've told the doc what I need is a nice, relaxing massage. He's sending someone round,' said Rex.

We called in the following week for a progress report. It turned out the NHS physio was less of a gentle-rub-with-essential-oils practitioner, and more like the bloke who ran basic training in *An Officer & Gentleman* who beasted Richard Gere from Arizona to breakfast-time. A physical workout which Rex said left him feeling a good deal worse than he did before, as he quietly took his leave from the fitness programme.

I was once in a ward with a decent old cove called Chris, who was a farmer, and, like me, a reformed smoker currently experiencing a post-op shortage of lung. They brought scales to the ward and weighed him. 'What did you weigh when you were admitted?' they asked. '104 kilos, I think it was,' he replied. 'You're 102 now,' they said. 'Not bad,' Chris nodded approvingly, 'considering I've had half me insides pulled out'.

Questions

*Y*ears ago I was working the between Christmas and New Year office shift. Which involved rolling at 10:30 in the morning, wandering around the building looking for someone to talk to, going to lunch at noon, returning from lunch at 3, checking if I had any messages, ignoring any messages and then going straight home.

Unfortunately, news of my wonderful new regime appeared to have filtered upwards.

'Are you in tomorrow?' asked my boss's boss's boss.

"Possibly," I replied, guardedly.

'What time?' he persisted.

"Why?" I asked from my firmly entrenched position somewhere to the north of *intransigent*.

Not that I was being awkward, I really wasn't. But like at Prime Ministers Questions, I'd just like to be as sure as I can that a careless answer doesn't bring forth a nasty follow-up question.

It's not that I want to be deliberately obtuse, it's just where we end up sometimes. OK, sometimes I do want to be deliberately obtuse, just for the fun of it. Or as a mate from New Zealand puts it, 'Don't you ever give a bloody straight answer to a bloody straight question?' To which I would have to reply, "Well, that depends". Mind you, he is a policeman.

Scene: Railway station bar at Weston-super-Mare called *Off The Rails*, and rarely was a joint better named for its pissy punters.

Not the place you want to stay in for long, so I'm just in for a twenty-minute snifter to pass the time before my connection arrives and to take part in this, well whatever it was it wasn't a conversation, this exchange perhaps:

Man at bar: Is it raining?

Me: I don't know, I just got off a train.

Man: Is it raining?

Me: No, I just came in on a train, you see, I haven't been outside.

Man: No, you said?

Me: No, I.. you see I just came in from Bristol, got off here, under cover, waiting for my next train. I haven't been outside and I didn't look out of the train window, d'you see?

Man: Is it raining then?

Me: No, it stopped 5 minutes ago.

Now, regardless of the what I knew or didn't know vis-à-vis the rain situation, I am wearing a frankly bloody massive oilskin raincoat with integral storm cape, which has a studded split up the back to accommodate the riding of a horse should you come across one, and straps inside, lower down in the leg area, probably for further horseplay. Sandra advises me it's called a Drovers Coat, but we know it simply as my Clint Eastwood coat.

Man at bar eyed up my coat. Although he didn't remark on the absence of any rainwater on it, so perhaps he wasn't so bothered about the weather after all.

'Lovely coat, that,' he said.

"Thanks very much," I replied.

'Yes, really nice,' almost risking a heavy glass ashtray across his knuckles when I thought for a second he was going to give the material a feel. Like I said, it's that sort of a place. If there has to be violence then it's best you get the first and only strike in before running away.

"Cheers," I said, wondering how rude it would be of me to neck this beer in one and wish him a brisk farewell.

'Just the job, that is.'

"Uh, huh," I uh-huhed, aware that the conversation appeared to have stalled.

'Yes, I've been looking for a new coat and yours looks just the thing I'd be after. Lovely coat that is. Where did you get it?'

"Canada," I replied. Suddenly unconscionably gleefully glad that I'd stuck around till the end.

Whodunit?

*T*hese things I have learned from TV detective shows:

There are no successful investigators who live a happy, settled family existence and the whole thing plays havoc with your private life.

You're never quite sure until the last ten minutes who's going to turn out to be related to whom.

The most famous guest star that you spot in the opening credits is always the killer. Thus saving you the bother of taking 2 hours out of your life only to discover that the mystery person is someone who had barely 5 minutes of screen time up until then. I tried this foolproof system during the opening titles of the *Inspector Morse* prequel, Endeavour.

"There's your murderer right there," I said, "Anton Lesser".

The opening scene fades in and there's the unmistakeable Lesser. However, he's not looking particularly racked with guilt or bloody of hand. Dressed as he is in the uniform of a Chief Superintendent. Well, the scriptwriter's got his work cut out here, I thought. For a bit.

I have had to accept then that this system is not quite so watertight since the TV companies twigged what we were up to and took to casting faceless unknowns as heartless-deranged-bastard killers.

The opening of a knocked door by Party A who then exclaims an unsuspecting "Oh, it's you," to the unseen Party B will always, but always precede the messy slaughter of Party A.

The sidekick to the star cop should consider themselves fortunate to take the prat falls, do the dirty jobs and, above all, make the star look good by not being nearly as clever.

The corridors of production companies are littered with the corpses of sidekick cops who got above themselves and, to the surprise of the viewer, were given the unceremonious flick and replaced by a new, and initially less threatening face in the next series.

The young cop will always throw up at their first murder scene/autopsy.

If someone's murder has left them facially disfigured then I'll bet you a pound to pinch of arsenic that it ain't who you think it is.

These things I have learned.

Recently we had a builder in, installing some shelving in my office at home. Nice fellow Chris, we know him pretty well. Kept him going with tea and cake. When he left, Sandra remarked that he'd left footmarks on the carpet in the spare room. "What's he doing in the spare room?" I asked. "No reason to go in there."

Twenty minutes later, Detective Sandra walks me through the reconstruction. 'I took a slice of cake up to him. While he is eating the cake, which is quite messy so you can only eat it from the plate with a fork, he wandered across the landing and he was standing looking at all of the books that you'd laid out on the spare room bed until you could re-stack them on the shelves. See the footprints, here, here and here? They're consistent with someone standing at the end of the bed and looking at the books, and why would he be standing there? Because he had to stop work to eat the cake and he's interested in music and cricket like you are.'

The final thing I've learned from TV cop shows is that they have an awful lot to answer for.

Outing

*H*ollow-eyed wretches eye me up suspiciously as if I somehow know a secret way out of this charnel house. Their haunted gaze darts this way and that, always searching for an opportunity, an opening, *something…*

Families have set up camps on any available strip of floor space, and they overlap their neighbours' boundaries at their peril. They guard their meagre supplies fiercely, never taking their eyes off those in close attendance. People on dangerous, nervy, hair-trigger alert as they chew on ragged sandwiches and suck sugary sustenance through straws. Perhaps casting the odd, covert and jealous glance in the direction of those they perceive have somehow gained on them, maybe edged ahead in the survival stakes.

You sense there might be evil done here, outbreaks of violence over food or queue jumping.

The sound of a child crying is ever-present. Sometimes joined in a cacophonous wailing choir by others. The air is heavy with gloom and despair, with people wondering how they came to be here, how, if they had their time again it would all be so different. They wouldn't have come within a thousand miles of this hellish place.

The Superdome in New Orleans, right after Hurricane Katrina. Well, actually, it isn't. This is England, my friends, England. This is London. This is the 21st Century.

What on earth had happened to trigger this post-apocalyptic scene? I take out my notebook and approach a weeping woman. Our eyes had made the briefest of contact through her wretched fingers as she clawed at her face and I felt a whisper of empathy.

"Do you know what's happened?" I ask. "Was it. Was it, (gasp)…The Bomb?"

She stares blankly back at me, her mouth opening and closing but as near silent as makes no difference.

I move in closer and bend forwards, offering my ear to her dry, cracked lips. I take a brief look at her tear-stained cheeks and her miserable features wracked with pain and fear and drained of blood by the hopelessness of it all. She managed to croak out these words:

'You bloody fool, can't you see its half-term?'

For this is the scene in the basement activity area for pre-schoolers in The Science Museum. Or as it might be re-branded at this particular time of year, London's Very Own Lunatic Asylum With Integral Refugee Camp.

To be honest though, in a way this could be viewed as a gentle introduction to what goes on next door at the Natural History Museum where the main event drawing people in seems to be the queue for the dinosaur exhibition, oh, and the queue for the toilets. I saw people in the dinosaur queue faint with excitement on reaching the sign which advised them they had just an hour to go before they might gain entry. At a guess, from our vantage point high up the stairs, on the self-satisfied and roomy slopes of Mount Superior, some of these pitiful casualties had already been in line for 2 hours.

A super doomsday survival exercise for the kids, I'd say, and, in its favour, at least it wasn't a West End musical.

Shop

*I*n terms of what one has to do to get through this thing they call life, I'm not so good at the shopping side of things, which is to say I plough a rather narrow consumer furrow and I don't much care to stray from it. This was driven home to me the other week when I got a call from my bank's fraud prevention department. I was just back from Britain's premier electrical funfair store for grown-ups, Richer Sounds – of which more later – when I got the call asking whether I'd attempted a ten dollar purchase that morning from a clothing store in New Orleans. *Nah.* Or tried to spunk a couple of hundred up the wall at a mobile phone shop. *Get* outta *here, girlfriend,* I might have said to the fraud prevention lady but satisfied her curiosity with a simple *Nah.* What about £20.00 at Amazon? *Yep, that's one of mine,* I said. How about £9.80 at iTunes? *Guilty as charged,* I replied. *Can you see a pattern emerging here?* I asked. Certainly can, she replied. I'm guessing she's married.

Some years ago, I returned home from a trip to Richer Sounds with a new twin cassette deck (trust me, they were big in the old days, kids. Like the Buttoneer) and a shiny new amp/receiver thing which was so wondrously studded all over with such an impressive array of knobs and blinking lights as to make a chap reach for a tissue. I plonked them on the table and presented Sandra with the item with which I was most pleased: The Richer Sounds branded coffee mug which they had gifted me instore.

Back to Richer Sounds the other week, and after a little light bartering – which I'm rather uncomfortable with but, as in *Life of Brian* it seemed to be expected, so I joined in – and, price agreed, there was a bit of re-boxing and wrapping up to be done and as we exchanged the inconsequentials, I dropped in the story about the mug. Nothing. *I was so pleased with it,* I said. Nothing. Just a, How would you like to pay, sir? *Please give me a mug, please give me a mug, please, please, PLEASE, PLEASE, PLEASE give me a mug,* I screamed inside my head. Would you like another mug? *Oh,* got to act all surprised now, *well, that's very decent of you, can't wait to walk in with that tonight, hahaha.*

Once again, honours were stolen by a bit of old ceramic whose logo probably won't last more than 6 dishwasher months.

I'm lucky, in that Sandra does the weekly food shop and I go barely twice a year and when I do it sticks another ton on the bill, easy. Well, your proper Argentinian Malbec doesn't come cheap, you know, and as for that lovely little section in Sainsbury's with exotic and enticing jars and tins of treats and sweetmeats from the mystic east and other far-flung parts. You pay for what you get, that's what I say.

Still, I'm a little phobic about supermarkets since this episode from the dim and distant. I got the call from the GLW (Good Lady Wife), could you pop round to Sainsbury's? The boys are coming round for dinner and we've got nothing in and I need some other bits? *Sure,* I said.

The girl on the checkout looked up – with a knowing look if ever I saw one, and then glanced pointedly at my purchases, all lined up on the conveyor:

16 cans of beer

3 pizzas

2 boxes of tissues

All that was missing was a video of *Debbie Does Dallas* and, from memory, it was out of stock, although they *did* have *Shaving Ryan's Privates*.

Akip

*"H*ow are you then, mother?" I asked.

'Alright, love,' she replied. 'had a bit of trouble with my bowel though, so I'm booked in to see the proctologist.'

"Same one you saw before?"

'Yes,' she replied.

"He's a good doctor isn't he?" I said.

'He is,' she agreed, 'although his fingers are a bit too thick for my liking.'

Oh mother. Last time she came to stay with us, on the Saturday morning, Sandra asked, 'Is your mother up yet?' No. 'Eleven thirty?' she observed.

Now, my mum is an insomniac. She can be heard wandering about in the night, and sometimes she sleeps a bit late. So we left a note for her next to the kettle and went into town to get her the Freeview box which we'd promised her for the onset of digital televisual delights.

Back an hour or so later and no-one was stirring.

'You think she's alright...?' asked Sandra.

"She sleeps late," I shrugged.

'I think you should go and check.'

"I can't," I said firmly, "she might be getting dressed. You go."

We stood in the kitchen looking at each other, listening intently for signs of, well, in the most literal sense, signs of *life* from upstairs. We moved into the living room which is directly underneath the spare bedroom. I looked at Sandra meaningfully, she *had* to go and see. She started out, had just reached the bottom stair, and it was then that we heard the reassuring thud of foot on upstairs carpet. Shortly afterwards, mother appeared, clutching a handful of assorted ailment pills.

'Have you got a glass?' she asked, 'So I can take these pills?' I handed her a small tumbler and with the practised air and expert execution of an old hand, she snatched a bottle from the fridge, filled the glass with chardonnay and washed down the pills. 'What time's lunch?' she enquired, brightly.

Long time ago, Sandra and I had a full house for a wedding weekend. Sandra's dad had brought a friend, Vi. Vi who used to work in an East End munitions factory in the war. Vi who told stories that put hairs on your chest. Big day, hot day, at the wedding on the Saturday was followed by us all lunching well on a sultry Sunday. In the late afternoon I took the mildly protesting dog for a walk and came back with ice lollies and choc ices for all. Most were lolling about in the cool of the lounge, I handed out the lollies. "Where's Vi?" I asked. 'She's in the garden'.

I step into the garden, Vi is seated at the table. But her body is slumped, head pitched forward and resting awkwardly on the table. Oh, bugger, I think. "Vi?" I call gently, and then louder, up a notch each time. And then much louder, "VI?" More urgently now. I'm at her ear. Nothing. The ice cream melting in my hand. I touch her shoulder. She opens one eye, she smiles, 'Thank you dear,' she says.

Because often I sleep deep under the duvet, hidden from sight, perhaps with a pillow over my head too, Sandra has on occasion had to resort to poking me in what she has to guess might be my ribs just to ensure that I haven't carked it in the night.

The late sleeping mother scenario was one we'd also encountered with Sandra's dad one lunchtime. He and I had probably been up late the night before, overdoing our mutual enjoyment of malt whisky, stinking big cigars, and our favourite Frank Sinatra and Count Basie album. Finally, I went up to check on him. Peered at him, bent over him, touched his face, and was *this* short of doing the misty mirror test, when one eye sprang open, 'I'm not dead, you know,' he announced, happily, 'not yet.'

Fugitive

I recall that years ago Sandra bailed out of the film *Jackie Brown* in the early stages, while I made the mistake of sticking with it. More recently, we both rued our decision to give the benefit of the doubt to *The Black Dahlia*. This truly dire tilt at *film noir* has – apart from Scarlett Johansson's shrink-to-fit sweaters - nothing to commend it, and I should have known that any film which pins the name 'Bucky' on a main character and not on a 4-legged furry sidekick with a wet nose wasn't going to pan out well. And let's face it, Lana Turner over Scarlett any day, right?

On a long-haul flight having had the gin and the food and the wine and the extra wine and read the paper and the magazine and started the book which I soon realised I wouldn't be sticking with, I plugged into the, ahem, in-flight entertainment system. Now, I don't much like watching films on aircraft because the sound's rotten and picture's too small and there are too many distractions, but I opted for *Quiz Show* which told the true story of how a quiz show (there's a clue in the title) was fixed in favour of the contestant who the producers felt would be the more attractive option for the viewers – the rich and handsome Charles Van Doren.

But didn't it go *on* about it? I think afternoon tea might have arrived halfway through, which always upsets my concentration, and then the headphones started to irritate, and as I had no idea when I'd started watching it and no inkling as to how long was left until we were to find out whether the fix would be uncovered and if Van Doren would admit all, I pulled the earphones out and went back to my book. Only to look up 5 minutes later to see the rolling of the credits.

Sandra pulled a similar trick on a trip we made to Australia in 2005. On the London to Bangkok leg she was watching the mumsy-back-street-abortionist-gloom-fest that was *Vera Drake*. She fell asleep though, missed the ending – so picked it up again on the Bangkok to Sydney leg, and promptly fell asleep again. Luckily, it was on again on a subsequent flight and this time she stayed awake right up until the time when they switched off the in-flight entertainment system.

This happened on the next flight too, and in all she had 5 goes at it. The ending was at last revealed a while after we'd arrived home when she was able to watch the last 10 minutes on Sky Movies, and, incidentally, wished she hadn't bothered.

The Fugitive starring Harrison Ford. "I'll stick a tape in," I said, for this was in the days when films were interrupted by News at Ten, the local news and 'the weather for where you are', and then the bloody weather again except this was 'the weather for where you aren't'. Followed by a bunch of adverts and I'd lose interest long before the film came back. So we taped it. Picking up where we left off the next evening, ten minutes in and the phone rang and it was a marathon, so we sacked it and went back to it at the weekend – starting from the beginning again, reaching the point where we'd broken off before we had a power cut. Two days later we had another bash – 'we shall start from the beginning again' – we got to the break-off point plus maybe 10 minutes before a shot of Harrison hiding in a coat rack, I think, was replaced by those old black and white wobbly lines which signified the end of the tape. We've never seen the end of *The Fugitive* because we are not meant to, and since then have gone to great lengths to avoid it – if switching channels can be described as such, and I suppose it can if you can't find the remote.

Lodger

*N*o Keith Moon am I, but within hours of checking into a hotel room recently I had broken the toilet roll holder, knocked the chrome cover off a light switch, pushed the plug into the sink without noticing that the lever for extracting it had gone missing and so to enable the drainage of stubbly shaving water had to prise it free with the aid of a metal soap-dish which afterwards bore only slight traces of bendage.

I know, it's hardly furniture being superglued to the ceiling or the contents of the entire room being removed and being reconstructed to scale in the car park is it? Particularly as I had several goes at fixing the toilet roll holder. Rock 'n' roll, eh? It's been a long time.

In the course of hanging around on the morning that I was leaving I noted the presence of an iron and ironing board in the wardrobe and seriously considered ironing something just because it was there. Not that I did of course. Being someone who has been banned from ironing at home for many years due to being so ham-fistedly crease-crazy and crap at it.

Luckily, on that occasion, there was none of that business about my room not being quite ready yet and would I like to bugger off out of the sightlines of the receptionist until someone's managed to push the old Henry round, squirt some Harpic under the rim, and wipe down the TV remote. Once, Sandra and I arrived at a hotel in Bangkok, the hours spent on our door to door journey now well into double figures and it being five in the afternoon I thought *what buggery is this?* when we were told, 'Your room isn't quite ready yet.'

"That's completely…" I began, before the receptionist interrupted.
'So we've upgraded you to a suite.'

"… completely brilliant," I continued.

Sadly, the once ubiquitous Corby Trouser Press was absent. Thus depriving the weary traveller of hours of improvised fun. Although it should be noted that the Corby is nowhere near as good as you'd think it would be for heating up Cornish pasties or melting cheese.

So, once I'd reprogrammed the safe and checked that the previous guest wasn't the sort of prankster who might set the alarm for 3AM, there was little else to do but ponder on the uselessness of those tiny drinking glasses, surely good for taking a shot of medicine but for little else. Like those things they leave lying about your room which look like magazines but actually contain nothing but adverts, the business of hotel rooms and hotel operations is a puzzle wrapped inside an enigma hidden behind a riddle and bound behind an ad for men's shoes from the Pastel Coloured Bootees for Chinless Wonders range.

I've always wondered, but never had the balls to ask, why the act of booking someone into a hotel involves several thousand keystrokes and the sort of brow-knittingly serious expression that should be reserved for the exclusive use of the neurosurgeon. Do we really need 10 minutes of *Ratatataptaptappitytaptaptap* before the solemn pronouncement of the room number and the handing over of the sacred card key and that little booklet to put it in which you have to sign but nobody ever asks to see? I can only guess that some greasy snake-oil salesman sold every hotel in the world the same system. Just as soon as he'd finished with the airlines.

Last

*F*amously, when the ailing George the Fifth was offered a day out in the royal playground that was West Sussex, he replied 'Bugger Bognor,' and actually never got the chance to wiggle his toes in the sand, or if more accurate memory serves about Sussex beaches, stub his toes on the pebbles. Because those proved to be the last words he uttered.

Now, despite the significant date at the time of writing, and my early mention of an unelected head of state, this is not to be a Jubilee-themed episode. It's also not really about famous last words or epitaphs picked out on tombstones, although Spike Milligan's always bears re-telling: 'I told you I was ill,' he said. In passing.

There's a wonderful episode of Hancock where Sid and Bill visit the lad himself in hospital where he is laid up with a broken leg. It plays on the fears of the patient, the clumsy conversation of the visitor and the boredom of both.
'Have you had your liver examined?' asks Sid, before going on to inform Hancock that he looks, 'What's the word Bill? Ashen. That's it, you look ashen.' Fair reminds me of coming out of hospital recently and being told that I looked 'gaunt'. Gaunt, if you please, summons up images of skinny, bony and all grey, papery-skinned and knocking on death's door. For gaunt is latter-day Peter Cushing isn't it? Peter Cushing on the Atkins Diet.

Personally, since that bout of surgery, I put a pound or fourteen back on soon enough, and, the fact I found myself briefly without the mid-years belly swell, might lead me to recommend major surgery and the prolonged bout of enforced hard-core dieting that pancreatitis brings you. However, that would be daft.

Rather reminds of my father-in-law, on exiting the consulting rooms where he had been given the dread diagnosis of lung cancer, he turned to my wife, Sandra, and uttered the immortal words, 'Give us a fag'.

Although perhaps immortal's the wrong word.

Talking as we are about The End, The Finish, the Big Sleep, I've been reading a collection of Alan Bennett's writings where he recalls attending the funeral of Miss Shepherd, the lady who lived for many years in a van in the garden of his North London house. Her Catholic farewell was the same as that of a friend of ours in that it was shoehorned into the usual weekday service. Hence sharing the pews with a bunch of strangers and, worst of all, being expected to engage in the RC call-and response thing they do – but by keeping schtum it's actually a breeze to avoid – and then they do this celebration of fellowship thing where one is expected to turn to the person next to you and shake their hand. Well, in my case, although the people looked over in expectation, as they were a good few feet away and I certainly didn't want to shake hands, I resolved a potentially awkward situation by giving them a little wave. And then folding my arms.

Now is the end. This is the end. It might not be, let's hope not. Let's remember two who are still with us. Val, who at 91 had a pacemaker fitted. 'It should last about 6 years,' said the doc. As Val replied, 'Not really going to affect me is it?'

And only last week an intensive care nurse stepped away from the patient and said to me, 'Do you want to hear what she just said?'

"Go on," says I.

'She said, I'm reading a really good book at the moment. So I hope I don't croak before I've finished it'.

Say

*A*s I can't bear to give Chris Evans an outlet for his inanities, having an aversion to sharing breakfast-time with egomaniacs being one of my more sensible traits, and I don't reckon 5-Live since it moved to Manchester, nothing against Manchester, well actually yes, something against Manchester, anyway, this means the default station in the mornings nowadays is Radio 4.

Now sometimes it pisses me off so much that I find myself jumping in ahead of John Humphries and interrupting the guests myself. Particularly if they're a rulebook-spouting timeserver or are hooked up in some we-know-what's-best-for-you-do-goodery, or a slippery, question-dodging politico. You'll understand that I can find it irritating, but at least they never say the most life-sapping words in radio, 'Give us a call, and let us know what *you* think'.

When radio opened up in the Seventies with the advent of commercial stations, for a few glorious years London's Capital Radio was a tremendously good radio station. Now, I fully understand the curl that your lip is adopting, given how bleedin' awful it's been for years, but back then it really was the polar opposite of playlist-driven, computer-operated pap by pollsters for pillocks and poseurs. The other London station LBC, was a speech-based affair. Offering an alternative take on the news to that of the BBC? Maybe that was the pitch, but in reality the listener was carpet-bombed with phone-in shows.

A bloke called Brian Hayes was LBCs top phone-in presenter. Obviously he achieved this status by being the most short-tempered and rude. Robbie Vincent was the BBC version. Nowadays it's Jeremy Vine who has me dashing for the off-button so to avoid even a second of his *bombastardry*.

A few years back I was interviewed on a local radio station about my novel, *None of your Business*, and when we were done the presenter asked me if I'd be interested in a regular spot. 'Oh, yes,' I thought.

They went on, 'It's a section we call *Have Your Say,* people ring up and…' 'Oh No,' I thought. Good for promotion and possibly book sales, although we shouldn't forget the reverse is also a possibility, but I decided that I just couldn't bear it. Tell us what you think. Or don't. That would be better.

'Have your say'. 'Tell us what you think'. Why? Why the thoughts of some crane driver from Walsall – sorry crane drivers, sorry Walsall – and not the thoughts of someone who might know what they're talking about, who might have something of value to impart? I'll tell you why, it's because if ever anyone rings up and has their say and the presenter twigs that this person is their intellectual superior by several million gigahertz and has the potential to flog them ragged on this particular subject, you can guarantee you'll hear these words quick-smart, 'Sadly that's all we've got time for'.

Old

I was earwigging on the conversation between my wife Sandra and my sister Helen which was taking place behind my back, so I was well placed to deal with the suggestion when it came moments later.

'Guess where we're going in June?' said Sandra.
"Where?" I replied, playing along.
'The Isle of Wight festival,' said Sandra.
"Have a nice time," I replied.
'You're coming too,' she protested.
"Not a chance. You both want to go because neither of you have ever done the camping out at a festival thing. I have. And that's precisely why I'm not doing it again."

Her crest was truly fallen, but my reasons were sound. I don't like big crowds of people these days, I don't think music works nearly as well outdoors as it does inside, and the idea of living and sharing 'bathroom' facilities with a bunch of strangers fills me with creeping BO and instant constipation. Sadly my abiding memory of the festival experience isn't some wonderful set by a legendary act, or going into any sort of mind-bending trance, nor engaging in acts of free love behind the portaloos. The word that comes to me when I reflect on the whole festival trip is *ordeal*.

Increasingly I'm finding that things are too late, too uncomfortable, too crowded, too noisy, or too cold, too hot, too wet and too windy. There is also about me now an air of prickly belligerence which means that my first stance about, well anything really, is "I'm too old to put up with all that nonsense". I find quite the best thing about getting older is that I no longer feel obliged to attend all sorts of things that in the past I would have done, simply because I was too timid to say, "No thanks." And the answer to any follow-up? "Why not? Because I don't want to."

On the downside, my knees ache, and it's a crushing feeling now when you've gone back downstairs only to realise that you haven't brought with you what you just went upstairs for and are going to have to go back again. Only last week I said to handily placed 6-year-old, "Do me a favour, go upstairs and get my phone." She wasn't too happy, and at first refused, but it's reassuring to know that a casual financial bribe still works. Or as we call it, pocket money.

Sandra was teasing me about something as we lounged about in front of the TV the other day, and my initial thought was to dive onto the floor, grab her feet and tickle them until she begged for mercy. But I thought it over and realised that hitting the deck was all very well, but I should also give a thought to having to get up afterwards.

Grow old, think ahead, stay off the floor and away from festivals. Perhaps not much of a life plan, but it'll do for now.

Someone gave me gardening gloves for Christmas, and I was delighted. I don't listen to a lot of music radio now, but when I do it's often Classic FM. These days I've got quite a bit of Sandra's Barbra Streisand collection on my iPod and one of my secret pleasures is listening to Barbs giving it loads on *Woman in Love* through the headphones while I travel home on the train. Another secret pleasure is listening to Kate Bush's *Sensual World* while on the train, although perhaps that should have remained under wraps.

Devil

*R*ecently I heard the creepy Son-of-Satan film, *The Omen*, described as being weak and rather silly. Not if you were watching it years ago when it was first on telly on the night of a massive thunderstorm. The storm grew ever closer, ever louder on this steamy summer night as my girlfriend and I sat in the dark watching Damien doing his dastardly devilish deeds. All of the windows were open and it seemed that when the thunder cracked we could feel it pulse through the air right into to our bones. Black as Old Nick's heart outside it was, so when a lightning bolt spat from the darkness it was threatening, blinding, it lit up the room in a way that's long gone since the invention of the energy saving light-bulb.

And at Damien's denouement, his fiendish finale, well, to be honest I don't remember much about the film, or the ending, but I assume he lived on in a sequel to tussle with truth, toughs and toothsomeness. What I do recall is my girlfriend taking off like Usain Bolt at first sight of the credits and calling back down the stairs, "Ha ha, now *you'll* have to put your hands outside to close the windows." I did too. The goosebumps which have just popped up on my arms are testament to the memory. Weak and silly? I didn't think so.

OK, to put it into some context, they were describing *The Omen* as weak and rather silly in comparison to *The Exorcist*. Now, speaking as someone who has always been far too terrified to go anywhere near *The Exorcist*, I'll have to take their word for it. People actually died in cinemas watching *The Exorcist* when it first came out, you know. They did too, it was in the papers.

I was reading Dante's *Inferno* the other day. Well, to be accurate, I was reading *about* Dante's *Inferno* on Wikipedia. What puzzles me, is that we are taken through the circles of hell where people are doled out nasty eternal punishments for their earthly sins, and believe me, judging by what goes on as one descends further, it's quite the holiday camp in the Third Circle for the gluttons - lying in vile slush and being lashed by ceaseless, foul, icy rain.

Although they are guarded by the great worm, Cerberus, obviously in the days before he was in the pay of the big salt companies. Virgil gives him the slip by filling his three mouths with mud. Little tip for you there, should you ever need it.

But what I don't get, is what's going on right down at Hell's business end. Because down there, actually in one of Satan's mouths and being gnawed at by the Devil's own gnashers and scratched and scraped by his foul claws is Judas Iscariot. But surely, Old Nick would be entirely in favour of the deeds of old Judas and be the first to give him a hero's welcome, a ride across the Styx in the Royal Barge, a slap on the back, buy him a pint and a fancy lunch, and lend him 30 quid plus a tenner for his trouble, wouldn't he?

And, anyway, I thought God was all about forgiveness. Or is there one rule for them at the top and one for the rest of us? Surely not.

I read Wiki's explanation of the Evil One's reasoning and, funnily enough, found it to be a bit thin. I'm sure someone could explain it to me. A passing Jehovah's Witness perhaps?

Well, I'll be buggered, here's one now.

Talk of the um…you know…

Popping

I'm just popping out.

As Terry Collier said in *Whatever Happened to the Likely Lads?* about his ill-fated marriage to Jutta, they had communication problems because he certainly wasn't going to learn German and all she picked up in English were a few handy phrases like *Where are you going? What time will you be back?* and *Have you got any money?* While it's clear to me at least that all Terry wanted to do was pop out every now and again.

Weddings are generally a fine excuse for popping out or indeed popping off somewhere. For, even in the presence of a free and open bar, men cannot resist the wicked lure of the pub across the road from the 'do'. 'Why do you want to go somewhere else?' the women will ask, resigning themselves to dancing to *The Grease Megamix* with each other or the bloke in the unfeasibly tight trousers who fancies himself as a bit of a ballroom Casanova.

It's irresistible though, because as I recall, the best times I've had at weddings have been the ones when I'm not actually at them, At a posh end of the wedding spectrum a few years ago, as we were ushered out of the church I sidled up to a brother-in-law and said "Come on, let's pop off for a pint". 'Aren't they doing photos?' he asked. "Do you want to hang around here for half-an-hour until you're called up to stand at the back behind some lass in a big hat. Thought not. Come on, there's a lovely old pub just round the corner."

Which is where we stood moments later, a foot on the rail and pints of guest ales in hand. Gentlemen, start your engines. In an instant a fellow guest burst through the swinging doors. 'Come on,' she announced, 'there's a taxi waiting'. "What about the photos?" I enquired, as weakly as I could manage while scarfing down a pint of ESB. Photos? Turns out they'd had them done in the morning. Thus pissing on another great tradition. Photos after the service please, and take as long as you like so we can all have a break. It's not all about you, you know.

I know it's an old film, but if you're ever considering giving *The Accidental Tourist* a go, well, don't. The main character – might be Geena Davis, but I can't bear to look it up – is kooky and, well, that's enough, isn't it?

We sat in the local arts centre watching this piece of crap and 20 minutes in I turned to my companion and said "I'm just popping out for a minute." 'You OK?' she asked. "Bathroom," I replied. So, out of the theatre, through the foyer and the front door like Will o' The Wisp, pub, pint, fag, jukebox, idle chat with the barmaid, thank Christ for that. Back to the theatre. 'You OK,' she asked. "Oh, you know," I replied, "not really. See you in a minute. Sorry." 'Hello again', she said, 'same again is it?' Pint, fag etc, and back in time to just miss the end of the film.

When Sandra and I first got together, a brother-in-law called round one Sunday morning. You know, at about 10 minutes to opening time. "I'm just popping out with Mike," I said. 'OK,' Sandra replied, with an expectant look. "Oh, I'll be an hour or so," I replied.

So I was somewhat sideswiped when I returned and a layer of ice had formed over the roast beef. But at least we'd got this technical issue understood and out of the way nice and early. When I said I'm popping out and I'll be an hour or so, Sandra used to think it meant I'd be an hour-and-ten-minutes, whereas what I actually meant was, I'd be at least ninety minutes and quite possibly a good deal longer. Thankfully nowadays I have more in the way of both manners and sense. Also, no happy accident this, the same number of testicles with which I was born.

Turn

"Could you do me a favour?"

There are few things that chill the blood like that seemingly simple request. A one-stop shop of do-goodery and no return. But...this may not turn out to be a one-off. People go on holiday, ask friends to take in their dog, and friends oblige, hosting lively mutt for 14 nights ('Could you make it 15? We get back very late on the Sunday...do you know we looked everywhere in duty-free and they just didn't have any scotch at all? Maybe next year'.) For, there will be a following year, and this is the first year where the request isn't even made, it's taken as read. 'We'll bring him round on Friday with his bowls and toys. Don't forget he *loves* a good long walk first thing in the morning and last thing at night, lunchtime too if you can manage it – but we don't want to impose, it's only because we know you love him nearly as much as we do. One more thing, he's got a terrible upset tummy, so we find it's best to let it harden off before you try and pick any up – let's hope for some hot weather eh?'

Then you're mired in something, in this realm of not wanting to let anybody down, because you said you would – and the thing with other people's dogs, like other people's kids, other people can't quite believe that the rest of the world might not be quite as keen on the apples of their eye or the fruits of their loins as they are.

Although, in fairness, these are minor kindnesses, at least in comparison to what goes on in *The Godfather*. Where the abusers of the undertaker's daughter are semi-killed by the Corleone family in retribution. In return the undertaker is presented some weeks later with the bloody remains of Sonny

Corleone who now looks much less like James Caan and more like a giant colander full of raw liver. The undertaker is instructed that his favour to Don Corleone will be to make his son look good so his mother doesn't have to see him like this. Like they say in sports interviews these days – that's a big ask.

A friend of a friend was going through a rough time. Really rough. As he drove along the M4 he mused on his mounting problems – the affairs and the break-up of his marriage, the bad deals, the business failures, the increasing pressure from the bank and from his creditors, the bailiffs, the brushes with the law, the boozing. A light bulb snapped on over his head, and he realised what it was all about, what had happened to cause this meltdown. 'This bloody Range Rover,' he said to himself, as he whacked the dashboard with both hands, 'This bloody car, everything was going fine until I bought this sodding car. Right, that's it – everything changes as of now!'

He veered onto the hard shoulder, jumped on the brakes, leapt out and grabbed a petrol can from the boot. He doused the jinx-mobile in gasoline, dropped a match on it and retired to watch the end of his nemesis from the embankment. As he lit a soothing fag, another vehicle screamed to a halt, a man jumped out with a fire extinguisher, put out the flames – and walked up to our friend with a grin on his face, 'I think I caught it in time, that's got to be worth a tenner hasn't it?' he said proudly and with outstretched hand.

Spiders

*L*ook he's crawling up my wall. Black and hairy, very small. Except, while he is undoubtedly black and hairy, he could not be described as being very small. Or small. An eight-legged creepy-crawly who, at first sight, is wearing cherry red Doc Marten's. The classic eight-eyelet, bovver boy Doc, of course.

Size matters here, you see. I gather up the smaller ones in my hands without a care, if they've graduated to senior school I may employ a bit of kitchen roll, but there's a certain size above which I will not go without safety gear. For the full-grown adult female, the only way is a pint glass, perhaps part-filled with water so that the vicious bastards are weighed down and cannot fight back.

It's odd that I'm more, well, I wouldn't use the word *scared* here, more *perturbed* by spiders when they're actually in the house. I'm not particularly bothered when they're in the garage or the garden, indeed it's common to return from a trip to the compost bin to find that a brush with an overhanging tree branch has deposited something tarantula-like about my person, which I brush off or re-deposit webwards with a gentleness that wouldn't be apparent were I in armchair or bath.

We've got it easy though in this country. I remember the Giant Steak Sandwich Eating Spider of Kenya and its 12-foot web like it was a horror film, and as for Australia...

Many years ago, and this is B.S., or Before Sandra, I was touring Tasmania with a young lady companion, and we stopped for the night at a place where you could rent a static caravan for the night. Before wine and dinner I was advised that, 'You're not coming anywhere near me until you've had a shave and a shower'. So, suitably primed, I headed off for the big wooden washroom cabin which was in the middle of the camp. They gave you a torch at reception, but as the camp was almost deserted it was a pretty lonely walk.

I pushed open the door and switched on the light.

The sound of innumerable webs twanging as their occupants sprang to attention, and the sight of these seriously dangerous things wall-to-wall among the rafters was most unnerving, but not so much as what happened next. I flicked on another light and rounded the corner to the washbasins where I saw a massive spidery lump of fangs and hair and legs-as-thick-as-your-fingers belting over the basins until it stopped, veered left and scampered underneath.

"Oh crap."

Now here's a dilemma. 'You haven't shaved.' No. 'Why not?' Well, there was this spider...

You'll understand that a gentleman has no alternative in such circumstances. So, I stood as far away from the basins as arm's length would allow, and I shaved. Not particularly accurately as my gaze was most often employed towards the underside of the sinks to check for attackers, but I shaved. I showered too, but that's less of a worry as the snakes tend to keep the showers free of spiders.

However, a friend topped my story. She has family in Oz who have a farm way out in the Queensland bush. She told us of going into rooms in the farmhouse and being assailed by dirty great spiders jumping out at you. Think about that for a moment, spiders jumping out at you. Think about that when you next spy an innocuous British spider cowering up there in the corner minding his own business. Never did anything any harm, did he? Well, apart from those flies…

Orders

*T*here was a moment this week when my workload stalled. The way it works, you see, is that Sandra will say something like, 'You know it's bin night?' and I'll nod and make a start on the ever-multiplying number of recycling crates and kitchen caddies and wheelie-garden-waste bins. Here's the thing, *while* I'm doing my bit for the planet, she'll follow up with, 'Are we having a fire tonight?' which is code for, 'Please light the fire'. And while I'm doing *that* I'll get the nod that the heavy cast-iron griddle pan needs retrieving from the bottom of the stack of other pans, and while I'm doing *that* there's no chance to draw breath because as Sandra cooks she calls over her shoulder and makes me aware that she could do with some grated cheese or chopped herbs for the dish.

Now, cunningly, although I'm not sure how I managed it, or if I could grate cheese in secret again, but I'd actually finished all of my allotted tasks before being lined up with another one. The old man being short of a task rather upset the system, as if leaving a gap would allow independent thought and action.

After dinner, I disappeared to my office for a bit – as it happens it was to do some work on Volume 1 of the book of the best of these pieces for *Why The Long Face?* You are currently reading Volume 2, which I hope you bought. Anyway, came down at about 10. 'You look tired,' said Sandra. 'You're working too hard.' I'd almost flopped into the armchair when she followed up expertly with, 'Before you sit down...'

Years ago we were doing up the house. A new fireplace had been put in and I had to cut and carve some new skirting board to fit around it. We were approaching the end of a long stretch of working at day jobs, and then on the house at evenings and weekends, and at last just a few tasks remained.

The skirting, some painting, and a light fitting to put up. We'd worked all weekend, it was late on the Sunday evening, "I've had it," I said. "I'll do the skirting tomorrow night."

Of course Monday didn't go to plan and I was late back from work. 'The skirting board?' she enquired. "Tomorrow," I said firmly. "No, I'm out tomorrow, Wednesday definitely." On Thursday morning, I said, "Tonight, I promise, I'm going to finish early, I'll have it done tonight without fail."

Got home early, got the tools, the wood, the bench out of the shed. I had to chase a bit of wood out of the skirting to slot into where the fender met the wall. Set up the bench, measured up, marked off, tucked the pencil behind my ear, I was poised with the chisel when I heard this:

'When are you going to put that light fitting up?'

Jokerman

*B*eing a bunch of blokes together in the public bar, we were all well aware that one of our number, Tim, had discovered a lump on his hip. We'd get running reports and updates and viewings. 'It's getting bigger Tim,' someone would say, 'You'd better get it looked at.' But, being a bunch of blokes in a public bar – albeit 25 years ago – visits to the doctor weren't really on the agenda, toughing it out was the way, as was having a laugh.

Eventually, though, ever-expanding lump and mounting discomfort took Tim off to the doctor where the word was that the growth had to be removed. Cue much gallows humour and jokes about anaesthetic. Although I thought *no sense, no feeling* applied more to the person who said it.

Tim was of course expected to attend the usual public bar proceedings, operation that day or not, after all, it was only a local anaesthetic, wasn't it? And there he was holding court at a large corner table, answering questions, showing his dressing, peeling it back a bit, fag in mouth, to reveal bruising and stitches. 'Did you see what *the thing* looked like?' someone asked. ''Course,' Tim replied, 'asked if I could have it. Roger's got it behind the bar if you want to see it. Rog..?'

Roger, the landlord appeared with a jar of murky liquid in which sat a gristly clump of ugliness. It was passed round the table, peered at, shaken, turned upside down – ragged trails of tissue fanned and fluttered about in the soup. The jar passed to Dale, who brought it close to his face, reached up and unscrewed the lid and – to calls of protest – dipped his fingers in. He pulled the lump out and took a large bite, chewing hard and finally swallowing with a satisfied smack of the lips. Then he bit into it again. Of those of our number who rushed to the gents, I can say that at least 2 of them threw up. Which was daft really, as the whole thing had been cooked up by Tim and Rog and Dale, and the jar contained nothing more than a pig's knuckle.

Now, this was a gag which had a bit of everything. The build, the drawing-in, the twist, and *both* vomiting *and* laughter to finish.

I'm reminded of an evening when some guests had been delayed. Now, someone who was at the time attached to one of the late arrivals sported one standard sized and one very large eyebrow, so much so that it was hard when talking to them to concentrate on anything else. I'm not proud of this but would say in my defence that cold drinks had been taken and anyway it wasn't me who came down from the bathroom having drawn on their own brow a huge, threatening Amazonian caterpillar of a growth which fair dominated their entire visage. In some kind of indelible pencil. As the laughter died down and the clock ticked towards to arrival time and there was no shifting this amusing artwork, the laughter built again. We tried everything. It wouldn't budge The phone rang, they wouldn't be long now, as the hysteria built, we howled until it hurt. Someone held him down as we scrubbed at the vile thing, nail polish remover was poured on his head as I toyed with a lighter. Eventually, scarred, reddened, and raw, there was a knock at the door.

This one contained an important element of comedy, which is danger. Although I'd say if you want to encounter real peril, try sharing the odd domestic secret in print.

Fizz

England won the Ashes a while ago. Celebrations were in full glorious flow on the TV and I beetled off to the freezer and popped the cork on the bottle of champagne which I'd placed there a couple of hours previously.

The GLW gave me the full blast of the old stink eye and said, 'I was saving that for a special occasion'.

"It may have escaped your notice, shining light of my existence, but this is a bleedin' special occasion. Now you'll have to excuse me, I must phone someone in Melbourne. Although he's been a bit hard to get hold of lately."

Funny how champagne is the drink most associated with celebration when a lot of people that I know would, when at a shindig or jamboree, generally prefer to raise a glass of good cheer as long as it's filled with something other than the old fizz.

Now, as someone whose default drink is a pint of bubble-free English ale, I am keenly aware of the pitfalls which lurk ahead for someone who is maybe used to kicking off proceedings with a few foaming tankards of something no more dangerous than about 4% alcohol. This party, having switched to the fizzy stuff for reasons of politeness or for a change or whatever, all of a sudden finds that when one pitches in to drinking Dom Perignon's finest at the same pace and volume as pints of beer, then there are head-swimmingly hard times ahead and really quite soon. For this reason, at one regular social event I steer clear of the champers and our host is always good enough to tip me off as to the location of the ale so that while all the rest are engaged in the tipping of the magnums, I can poodle off and help myself to something far less dangerous.

I found this pernicious brew can also replicate the feeling of a sock full of sand on the back of the unwary bonce at other times.

Take a tip. If starting the evening with it might be a bad idea, winding up a night at a rugby club dinner with it is an even worse one.

I reflected on this at 3AM as I was forced to abandon my billet in my hosts' dining room where the blow-up bed was pitching and tossing like it was in a force 8 and crawl on my hands and knees out of the French windows to be sick in a drain. Ah, happy days.

My brother-in-law, Mike and my sister were invited for lunch at the house of a friend who'd married a chap who was a rising star in the foreign office. Very old school tie, ra-ra red-trousered, jazzer type. 'Thought I'd have some fun with Simon,' Mike reported later, 'you know, get him at it, see what he was like pissed.' It's a plan, I suppose. However, something of a fatally flawed one. For the pre-lunch drink for all was champagne and it turned out to be a fool's errand for Mike when he ensured that the chaps' glasses were kept charged, and his amusing strategy came to grief on the twin rocks of upbringing and experience when the pissed-up Herbert in the corner trying to focus on his roast beef turned out to be our Michael. While Simon, of course, was practically weaned on the stuff.

Hat

*W*e were invited to Sunday lunch a couple of months ago with some friends who live some distance away, so were further invited to stay the night. We rose on Monday morning, descended the stairs as the aroma of freshly brewed coffee wafted out from the kitchen. Breakfast was on the go and our hosts advised us that as the morning was a chilly one, they had lit a fire in the lounge, also that they'd put the news on for me. Very nice too, lovely welcome. So it was rather ungracious of me to sour the mood by voicing my dislike of the female presenter of this breakfast news programme. What's wrong with her? I was asked. "She's false," I said, "although in fairness, the only person I dislike more than her is that bloke." Heads turned screenwards as the rather self-satisfied, shiny little man who reads out the football scores greased his way into shot. Ungracious? Yes, I'll admit to that, uncalled for etc., but was my dislike a rational one? Yes, it was. It irritates me that during Royal Ascot, which is a five-star meeting, featuring the very best of horses and jockeys and top class races, that the focus on this TV show is this person getting himself done up in morning dress at 6AM to talk about what people will be wearing and whether the Queen's going or not, and never mind some proper journalistic-style coverage of the racing.

But if we move into the realm of irrational dislikes, there are some queer ones about to be sure. My mother's blind to the charms of Cary Grant - and therefore I have decided I am probably adopted, or if my ma can't see the greatness in the best screen actor of all time I should like to be placed with a new family. She also spits fur balls at the sight of Gloria Hunniford, John Wayne, and the insurance ads featuring both the meerkats and the opera singer. I don't like Jeremy Paxman either, she said. "I do," I protested. Well, I knew *you'd* like *him*, she said, pointedly.

A colleague can't bear Frank Sinatra as she says he looks too pleased with himself, but she adores Robbie Williams – whose smirk is of course off the scale and in inverse proportion to his talent. At least Frank had the chops.

I have never seen *Friends*. People used to say they were like Joey or, one of the other ones, and I had not a clue. Reason? I could never get past that weedy theme song. Now and again I thought I'd give it a go, but as soon as these guitar-toting do-gooders said they were going to be there for me I decided it was time I was going to be somewhere else and sharpish. I don't care for the local TV weatherman because he wears brown suits, but the rest are probably too numerous to mention. Easier to ask me who I *do* like.

Sandra throws things at Fiona Bruce, little old wine drinker Jilly Goolden and Countryfile's Julia Bradbury. None of whom bother me. But when we sat down to watch *Zoolander* we glanced at each other after a bare few minutes and knew we had to re-think things. Reason? The spectacularly annoying Owen Wilson made his way onto the screen prompting a joint dash for the off-switch.

Mrs Bryer wins this one though. "Shall we watch The French Connection?" I asked. 'No, she replied, I don't like it.' "What do you mean you don't like it? What's not to like about The French Connection?" 'I don't like Gene Hackman's little pork-pie hat,' she said. And you can't argue with that.

Liar

*R*ecently, an office where a friend works rid itself of an employee quite suddenly. You know the scenario, an email comes out on the Monday informing everyone that so-and-so had left the previous Friday. Funny, I said to Sandra, my pal said they overheard one of the girls saying just last week, and before the departure, that she'd seen the soon-to-be-gone, and 'just wanted to give her a hug'. 'That's the person who got her the boot then,' said Mrs Bryer. Shocked I was at the duplicity, and more so at mine and my mate's naivety.

Why so shocked though? Because we all do it. When was the last time you called in sick to work when all you were nursing was a secret spring in your step? Or cried off from an unattractive invitation under some pretext? Or pretended to like someone's horrid house or frightful food or revolting children?

Unfortunately we can't come because my auntie just died, just a minute ago, actually I had to step over her to get to the phone, or the car's broken down, the trains are on strike – no, just the trains round here – some local thing, no, I don't think it's even made the news, or the roof blew off in that freak tornado you probably heard about it, mmm, that's right, two slightly injured, and a dog missing. I've had a recurrence of the Yellow Jack I picked up when I was kidnapped by pirates in the South China Sea.

See, it's easy. All you have to do is lie with conviction.

I overheard this phone call on the train just last week and scribbled it down as best I could:

'Hello? Is that Chris? Chris, I'm sorry but I'm going to have to cancel tonight. Sue's not well so I'm going to have to look after the little ones'.

So far so good, eh? Then he lost his nerve and blew it.

'What's *wrong* with her?' (....*insert fatal hesitation here*.....) 'We, er, we think it's a sort of a touch of mild food poisoning.'

Now, you couldn't blame the party on the receiving end of this steaming pile of ordure from a bull's arse if they'd said quite firmly, 'Oooh, you little liar'. Touch of a sort of food poisoning indeed. And *mild*, if you please. Oh dear.

In my experience, you've got to attack such impertinent questions as 'what's wrong with her?' with all forces at your disposal and damn the torpedoes.

'What's wrong with her? Well, she'd rather it was kept quiet but if you must have details it's actually Dengue Fever. That's OK, you weren't to know. Sorry I bit your head off, it's just a bit (...*now here's how to use a pause*.) stressful (swallows hard). Yeah, I know, she's in pretty rough shape, so it's....it's a ....worry. What? Oh yes, of course, she'd appreciate flowers, I'm sure.'

You're going to ask me what of afterwards? Of maintaining the charade? Easy. 'Well, we *thought* it was funny when NHS Direct said it was Dengue Fever so it came as no surprise really when it turned out to be food poisoning. Yeah... well, it *was* a worry at the time, still, we can laugh about it now..'

Badge

A few years ago, I was privy to a workplace final warning letter which was issued to someone who, in a peerless display of anarchic brio, announced he was going to the bank to pay in half-a-million quid's worth of company cheques, paused on the way out to pick up the keys to a company car to which he had no entitlement whatsoever, and wasn't seen in the office for 2 days. On his return, he did his best to brass it out but was sunk by his inability to remember what he'd done with the cheques, and indeed what their current location might be. Ended up turning in his badge soon afterwards.

Ah, the workplace badge. The badge which some wear around the neck, even when they're not at work. I suspect there are those that wear it to bed so that they might give the company logo a goodnight kiss. Badges worn in this 24-hour-a-day fashion are generally seen around the necks of men who attempt to accessorize the business suit with a backpack rejected by primary-age kids, an orange cycle helmet and little fold-up clown's bike. Note to these men. It's not a good look. Although, astonishingly, you do lead another in the fashion stakes. That's the bloke who's dressed the same as you, helmet and all, but doesn't have a bike. No. He has one of those little silver kiddie scooters with which to push himself around town. Beep beep!

I'm reminded of a Friday lunchtime, when there was a gathering in the pub for someone's leaving do. It was in a town centre, so it was anyone's guess where he worked. Right up until about half-past-three when he tore off his company-branded tie, screwed it into a ball and shouted "Stuff

Northern Telecom!" Two things to note here, 1. Northern Telecom are no longer with us, and 2. He didn't say 'stuff'.

Half-an-hour later, he unclips his company ID badge and hurls that across the room, together with a further volley of vituperation directed in what he assumed might be the general direction of the Northern Telecom offices, although by this stage it was clear that he had little idea *where* he was.

I heard later that when he'd returned to a state of equilibrium, sometime the following Monday, that he came to realise the folly of such fiery, foolhardy badge-flinging. For he had forgotten that without the magic badge, as far as Northern Telecom were concerned, he fell outside the realm of existence and they cared not a jot about the stuff in his old desk. Or his coat. Or his car. All the man on the gate cared about was keeping this badgeless idiot on the *outside*.

Had lunch last week in a pub in Yorkshire. I nip off to the gent's, and pass a woman in a company name badge giving some earache to a female colleague as they troughed through their main courses. 'I'm going to be straight with you. We really need you to step up to the plate and prioritise..' she said to the poor wall-eyed wretch who clearly wasn't sure whether piling into the old haddock and chips was the response she should be offering, or whether she was expected to say something like, 'You can count on me boss, I know the location of every bit of low-hanging fruit in this motherfudging outfit.'

I paused, I leant in, "Excuse me?" I ventured, to the badge-flaunting battle-axe who dutifully arranged an expectant look on her chops. "Why don't you belt up and eat your chips?"

That would have been good wouldn't it? Except she'd probably have said, 'That's none of your business,' and then I'd have said, "Coincidentally, *None of your Business* is the name of a book you could do with reading.."

Snip

*"C*an we stop for a minute? I've got hair in my mouth."

When was the last time you said that? *Me* too. In the barbers, and just the other week.

I'd gone to a new place, you see, and so we had to have the introductory chat, which usually begins with the barber asking, 'Just finished?' and at the mid-point will feature me not being able to remember or decide whether to have it tapered or squared off at the back. I suppose I should take more of an interest because, let's face it, the back of my head is where it's all going on these days, hair-wise.

I'll often apologise for leaving it weeks too long and letting it get in such a state, finishing off by saying that my wife had insisted I need a haircut. 'Have you ever told her that *she* needs a haircut?' asked the barber. Which, well-worn line or not, was still amusing – despite the fact that Word Magazine's head honcho David Hepworth had Twitter-messaged me the same observation not 24 hours earlier. To which I could only reply with something along the lines of the subject taking us towards dark and treacherous waters for which we were inadequately equipped.

Turns out the barber gets hair in his mouth all the time, and in lots of other places. He said that when he gets home he strips off in the garage and leaves the pile of hairy togs which have seen him earn a crust that day on the floor as instructed by his very own Good Lady Wife. Then he's straight into the shower. 'Couldn't sit down to dinner otherwise, could you?' he said. And, thinking about it, eurgh, you really wouldn't want to, would you?

There was a young lad, 16 maybe 17, in the chair next to me, being trimmed up by my barber's twin brother, who was also dressed in the all-black uniform. Which, in a place which is full of mirrors, is something to really mess with your head. Had the boy decided about the front? He had, he would have the equidistant half-inch spikes. And suddenly I was glad that I had grown up in an era where short hair signified only that the bearer was in the army. The rest of us attempted either the Rod Stewart or the Rory Gallagher and there wasn't much choice of anything else, or more importantly, fashion didn't demand it.

I mean, I was no good at buying clothes – as evidenced by my Tesco Bombers, so thank the Lord that I didn't have to think too hard about haircuts. Get it cut about once every nine months and please God not too short. Because those who got the over-trim didn't half cop it at school for the next week or so.

I recall being in my first job and getting the barnet done at the weekend, thinking that the piss would be roundly taken by my new workplace chums, the only difference being that it would be so much worse than before. Because these were crueller and cleverer grown-ups. Of course, not a word was spoken, so I came to realise that a whole new set of rules applied.

As I sat in the barber's chair in the prime spot right by the window, with the barber's brother as his wing-man to the right and then a sizeable gap to the other fellah who occupied the far corner, I realised that here was another rule – barber shops, like bank cashier windows and post office counters must always leave at least 50% of positions unmanned and empty.

AMERICAN BARBER SUPPLY

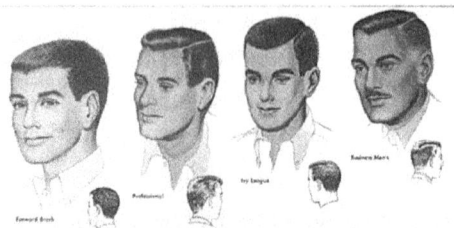

OFFICIAL HAIR STYLES for MEN and BOYS

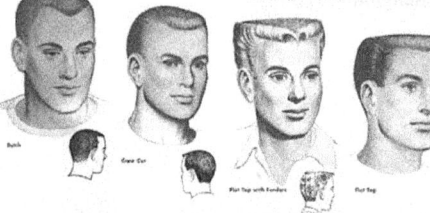

We specialize in cutting hair correctly... the way you like it

Fight

I'm not a violent man. But having said that, although completely unprovoked, I once whacked someone at school. Wandered up, all casual and I punched them. I'm not proud of it, particularly as I did it for a bet.

A couple of good things came out of it though. Firstly, I learned that hitting people on the side of the head with your bare hands *really* hurts your knuckles and can actually shift them out of their natural position – which is a bugger for a typist, which is what I find myself mostly doing these days. The second good thing resulting from this whole sorry episode was that I got away with it. Although I wasn't at school with Phil Collins so he couldn't have known or taken inspiration from this particular dust-up, but the getting away with it was truly against all odds.

However, it was back around the same period that I got my comeuppance for this shameful episode that I *almost* got away with. We're on the train, coming back from Spurs, and, to fill in some historical background, this is in the dark days of aggro when football visited casual violence on fellow fans and innocent bystanders as a matter of course and regularity.

There we were on the train. This is a while ago, so the train had a corridor. Down the corridor into our carriage came, ooh, a bunch, a crowd, of Chelsea fans. Maybe 8 of them. Heading back west like we were. They piled in and, well, looked at us. There were 10, perhaps 12 of us. Some of the more cowardly among our number (like me) were already casting looks about the carriage and performing simple calculations. Like, if one of them is hitting my mate Glyn, then he won't be hitting me as well. 'Who did you have today?' we asked. *'Newcastle'*. 'How'd you get on?' *'We lost 2-0'*. We balanced our delight at their rotten result with the prospect that because of it they might be keener on having a fight. What was this? I was terrified. I liked football, putting my scarf on, having a hotdog and onions outside White Hart Lane and buying a programme. I didn't want to fight anyone. I certainly didn't want to fight a large and possibly tooled up group of anyone.

A stand-off developed. They clearly didn't fancy the odds, but, being Chelsea fans and none too bright they hadn't twigged that despite our superior numbers there was not one fibre of our scrawny adolescent beings that fancied a scrap, a bloody nose and bruising instead of the bag of chips we traditionally had when we got off the train. Split lip with salt and vinegar? No ta. We dug in. It was quite impressive really, all playing strong and silent. Except Greenie, who we knew was ready to swap allegiance at the first drop of blood. *'Look at him'* the Chelsea ringleader said, nodding at me. *'Hard man, holding his balls'*. Yes, I was sat back in my seat, legs outstretched, thumbs in my Levi belt loops, and so with my hands in the inevitable cupping position. My chin on my chest – to stop my head from shaking. But I'll say this – it bloody worked.

There used to be a card school in my old local, as there tends to be from time to time, until people fall out over money. After being at work, I walked in early one Saturday evening, got myself a drink and sat down. *'Get us a drink,'* said the notoriously fiery Dobson, in the midst of a hand, chucking a tenner on the table. "No," I replied, "get your own. I've been at work all day."

'Get us a drink,' he persisted, *'I'm in a school.'* I'm afraid I said, and I remember it well, I said, "What did your last servant die of?"

You know what Dobson said? He said, *'Don't say that. Say that again and I'll itcha. Don't get me wrong, I like you. I don't want to do it, but I will itcha.'*

That last story tells you all you need to know about fighting and people who fight. What happened? I went to the gents and then hid by the juke box. One thing to be said for cards, they're a great distraction.

Happy

I see young Stephen Morrissey's got a book out. I've flicked through it and I can report that it's not packed with comic anecdotes about hijinks on the golf course with his showbiz pals. It's also many notches below the greatest autobiography ever written which is of course *Who On Earth is Tom Baker?* By Tom Baker. Actually there's not too much *Dr Who* stuff in it, which is all to the good, as I speak as someone who is genuinely baffled, addlepated, and perplexed as to why *Dr Who* would appeal to anyone over the age of, oooh, eight.

Right, one paragraph in and I've already upset Smiths and *Dr Who* fans.

I never liked The Smiths, nothing personal, I just think that when they started out in the old song and dance business that I was a bit too old for them. I'm sure if you first heard Morrissey's musings at, say, 14, then you probably loved 'em. I didn't. I never understood how people could get so excited about something so dreary.

Anyway, enough of The Smiths. I'll tell you who I do like. The Drifters. You want to know why I like The Drifters? Well, I'm going to tell you anyway. Because they're a group who like to get out and about. No moping around in the bedroom writing letters to the NME for them. They like to have a good time and then tell you all about it by way of the popular song. If they're not *Down at the Club* or *Under The Boardwalk* (down by the sea on a blanket with my baby), they're probably spending *Saturday Night at the Movies* or they might be *Up on the Roof* before returning to the local Odeon on Sunday where they'll be *Kissin' in the Back Row*. See? Fun times. On Broadway, see? Not like those miserable Four Tops forever mooning about and staying indoors in their *Seven Rooms of Gloom*.

For is there not enough misery in the world without having woebegone people sing it at you too? The current crop of guitar-strumming teenage wretches forever moaning about their lot while tearfully declaring their willingness to be someone's hero while sounding like they're wetting themselves in fear. *I don't care what they say,* they sing. Who are these *they* who crop up with boring predictability in the modern chart-bothering popular song, whose singers' profess not to care what *they* say. I can't see why they would keep banging on about the *they* if they're not that fussed about the *they*. And what they say.

Thanks to the splendours of Spotify I have also been enjoying an album called *Happy Music*. I was listening to it as I wrote these words. The Royal Artillery Mounted Band playing Happy Music. Cheers me up, you see.

Now, oddly, this brings us back to Morrissey. Because on the final page of his book, not only does he announce his intention to give sausage sandwiches another chance, he states his intention from now on is to concentrate on putting out nothing but Happy Music.

Now that's what I call a twist.

High

"*Y*ou mean if I just peg out some banana skins in the sun and leave them to dry and then scrape off the insides and roll them up in a Rizla, you mean it'll be just like smoking a joint?"

So said I all those years ago, but let me tell you, even though I cheated by trying to speed up the process by putting the banana skins under the grill, it was nothing like smoking a joint. Just as dropping an aspirin into a glass of coke didn't have the same effect as whatever it is that it was supposed to, indeed it had no effect at all apart from that on the poor soggy aspirin.

I once saw a small ad in the *NME* which promised to replicate in legal fashion those pleasures which were once only gained from an illegal source. In the name of research and curiosity I sent off a postal order and there came winging back by 2nd class post what I'm fairly sure now was a bag of dried oregano. By a strange and circuitous route I found myself some years later in a rather swanky hotel and being advised by the manager, no less, of the mind-expanding properties when smoked of another herb. He even showed me where to pick it. I cannot vouch for its effect on the synapses, but I can report that it gave me an awfully sore throat.

There's one more example of what I suppose we must call legal highs – but, as these days they seem to be at least as dangerous than their illegal versions.

Sandra and I once spent a morning in the botanical gardens on a day trip to one of Sri Lanka's cities, afterwards we visited the gift shop, or pharmacy. The man explained that they had all-natural cures for most things, and things for other things which might be of interest to the discerning gent. 'This bottle,' he said, 'contains an aphrodisiac.' He went on to promise improved performance and heightened pleasure from this bottle of fragrant oil. "How much?" I asked. It was a pound or so, I think. 'Just rub it on,' he said, 'then a little around the gums'.

Back from our trip and at the hotel I don't recall too much from the evening being improved or heightened, anyway we finished off the bottle in the morning. I had a beer or two on the beach a couple of hours later, and *that* was when I experienced some heightening of the senses. Among many other things, I jabbered on about the crazy shapes of the clouds, the amazing colour of the sea, and the all-round far-outness of our surroundings as I bounced around the beach – full of piss and vinegar and, well....

Later, I checked out the bottle we'd bought from the botanical pharmacist. It contained something to give it some fragrance – jasmine perhaps, but according to the label the main constituent part, apart from the oil, was cocaine.

Apart from anything else, Sri Lanka's such a long way away and anyway, try as I might I can't remember the name of the bloody stuff.

Sick

*O*bviously the last thing I want to do is bore you with tales of my ailments, but I had an attack of something rather unpleasant the other week that left me in a bit of tizz. Now, as this problem was related to my long-term lung condition and I was prepared to admit that I was suffering more than a tad, at 4AM when Sandra asked not for the first time whether I needed the doctor, finally I caved in and agreed. Although I was soon disabused of the notion that our friendly family GP would soon be bowling up the path with a cheery whistle and ready-warmed fingers. Instead, I got a rather distracted person on the 'phone whose prime aim in diagnosis was to avoid going anywhere on such a miserable night.

So, drenched in sweat and with my innards in the cruel grasp of the icy fingers of Beelzebub I resolved to wait the bastard out. After a painful few hours, and still rather nauseous and unsteady, I decided a change of scenery was in order and set up camp in the spare room. Sandra asked if I needed anything:

"Could I have my *50 Years of Private Eye* book please? And the one by Francis Wheen? No, not that one, the other one. *The Golden Age of Paranoia*. And those magazines that I left downstairs. Oh, and my i-Pod. Ah, sorry, not those headphones, could I have the others please? Yeah, they're downstairs where you just got the magazines from. Ooh, and I've run out of water. Thanks. Do you think one of your red bush teas would do me any harm?"

Great loss to the nursing profession my wife. Like Florence Nightingale if she'd trained with the SS.

After 48 hours of looking like I'd just been dug up, I began referring to the spare room as 'my day room' and my nurse – who was born with the extra share of the tidiness gene that certain other family members seem to be missing – my nurse was going quietly spare. Not at my, it must be said, pretty infrequent requests, but at the presence of two unmade beds in the place, and me insisting on flitting between one and t'other, like a Victorian damsel beset with an attack of the vapours.

At least nowadays the entertainment options for the sickly are a little more easily realised. Years ago, I was confined to bed with a prolapsed disc in my lower back. An episode of this meant total immobility for at least 2 days and on this occasion Sandra set me up before she went to work. She'd already been out and bought me a paper, which she brought up to our bedroom with a foil-wrapped sandwich, cigarettes, lighter, ashtray, books and magazines, paracetamol and morphine pills which Sandra's dad had given me. A little water and a cup of tea and we were almost set for the day. We had a TV/Video unit on the dresser at the end of the bed and a well-wisher had dropped round a selection of videos the night before.

Sandra organised my arrangement of pillows and I eased myself back, propped up now like some Eastern Potentate. 'Which film do you want?' she asked before she left. I chose one. "Just pop it in the machine," I said, "and I'll watch it later." She tossed the remote on the bed and went off to work.

I drank my tea and finished The Times. I rolled over in some discomfort to pee in the pink vase which had been left for such a purpose. Rolled back, and, ready for the film, chucked my book out of the way. Before I saw anything happen, I *heard* the tell-tale whirr and clunk of the VCR preparing to eject the tape. Seems I had managed to find the *eject* button on the remote without even trying. Ah well, she'll be back later. Only 9 hours to go.

Shortcut

It's a film. The character over there whom we know nothing about yet is introduced to the audience as being selfish, arrogant and deluded. He's smoking a roll-up of dubious provenance and at last we pan back so that a guitar case is revealed to be sitting beside him. This is the dramatic portrayal of the musician. They do the something similar when they want to signify a writer – except they substitute a half-empty bottle of scotch for the joint and a pencil sits in for the old banjo.

I realise that there are artistic factors at work here, and the director needs a shortcut to save two things. Firstly, time, and secondly, the audience having to think too hard when he wants them to be concentrating on his carefully designed tracking shot. But is it really necessary for the lawyer to always be the one who's in a tearing hurry? 'Sorry, I'm due in court', they'll gasp as they struggle with the hugest of humungous bundles of files underarm, papers spilling out, yet being caught by a handy and handsome-stroke-pretty passer-by when it's necessary to engineer a little love interest.

In the old days if you saw someone in a mac, in the pissing rain, lighting up a fag and looking for a pub that was open then that person was bound to be a copper, if he had an ex-wife and a boss who didn't like him, well that was the full set and he was obviously a very good detective, if not a very good husband or much of a team-player, but you marry the job don't you, love?

Journalists also ticked most of those boxes, but they tended to have bad teeth and a rather seedy air about them.

You want a loose-ish woman? Then get the wardrobe department to dress her in stilettos and a pencil-skirt. Make sure her highlights are overdue, she has a slightly knock-kneed walk and can hold a glass of gin at a 30 degree angle. Job done.

On the other hand, if you're casting a vicar he must have a big set of teeth that wrap around his chops like a corner sofa in white leather. Well, not really, but ever since Dick Emery played such a character that's what I expect from a vicar. To the extent that one of the experts on the *Antiques Roadshow* – the one with the large specs, the slightly greasy hair in a side-parting and, most crucially, the mouthful of teeth – is known round these parts as Dick Emery.

If a murderer's involved this will invariably be the loner, the outsider. The kids throw eggs at his windows, and he is what used to be called the local nutter. In fact, life imitates art here, as I believe there have been certain high-profile, real-life cases in which they've been so pressurised for a result, that the police still rely on this theory, regardless, or in spite of, or possibly because of, offender profiling like they have on telly. Which leads them to arrest the local oddball, even though he's likely to be freed on appeal in a few years when all the fuss has died down.

During a murder mystery we were watching, I said to Sandra, "Look, you can tell she's supposed to be a librarian, 'cause she's wearing glasses."

But my theory doesn't always hold true, as Mrs Bryer replied, "Wouldn't be the fact she's surrounded by shelves full of books then? In a big building marked *Library*?"

I never said it was foolproof, now did I?

Stewart

*F*or a brief, yet worrying period it seemed that our visit to Las Vegas would coincide with Celine Dion's residency at Caesar's Palace. Where she was going fifteen rounds with the American songbook and expected to have it bloodied, on the ropes and begging for the ref to step in way before the scheduled finish. Well, as Sandra's partial to a bit of old Saline Drip I would of course have swallowed hard, fronted up and taken it like a man. I'm sure I would have at least enjoyed the spectacle. Even with fingers jammed hard in each ear.

Anyway, Lady Luck stepped in and it turned out that the leather-lunged Canuck was on a break or having her yodel serviced or something, and the turn whose shift lined up with our stay would be none other than the world's most famous flag-waving, non-resident Scotsman (betting without Sean Connery, of course), the spiky-haired *Maggie May* hitmaker Rod Stewart.

So, there we were in the most intimate 3,000 seater I've ever been in, when Rod bounded out and scooted through The O'Jays old hit, *Love Train*. The exact same song that Gladys Knight opened with a few nights previously over at The Tropicana, cover version fact fans.

After the first number he announced that there was *exactly* an hour-and-forty-two-minutes to go because, 'They want you spending money in their casinos.' So, cleverly, immediately it's *us and them* with Rod on the side of *us*. Even though he's the only one who's on a huge wedge for the night. And 102 minutes from that point it was indeed all over. He added, 'Come up the front, take photos, whatever you want 'cos we're here for a party. Get on stage if you like.' A sentiment not shared later on by his security staff when a few brave young ladies took the plunge. One anecdote was flagged up as being, 'As unusual as me buying a round.' Happy to pose for photos mid-song with front-rowers, he was self-deprecating, charming and funny, and interacted with the band to the extent that when the backing singers had their moment in the sun he was content to stand stage rear and clap along unobtrusively. Or as unobtrusive as you can be in a an electric purple suit and leopard-skin brothel creepers.

There were a couple of costume changes and we had a bet on the final one, but there were no winners because he came out dressed as Frasier's dad, Marty Crane, in chinos and tartan shirt.

Not all of the set hit the spot for me, but thankfully, for every duffer there was at least one zinger to make up for it.

As for the punters, the was a heavy fan club presence down the front, and the rest veered from top-end raucous to those who got up only very reluctantly at the end or to attempt to catch one of the signed footballs which Rodders either punted into the balcony or, rather sweetly, tossed ever so gently into the first few rows. Assorted items of ladies' underwear were pitched onto the stage and generally given the once over by the old boy, together with, rather bizarrely, a high-heeled shoe.

It made me think that I should cease my carping that he stopped making decent records around 1975, or over his sleepwalk through The Great American Songbook and think of him simply as The Beloved Entertainer. And after his introduction of *The Killing of Georgie (Part I and II)* I could forgive him almost anything. 'This,' he said, 'is a long song, so it's probably your best opportunity to get a drink or go to the toilet.' Which, let's face it, is the sort of essential information that most gigs are lacking.

Titfer

I took a hat to New York years ago, middle of winter, but I found that I was too self-conscious to wear it. Until Mrs Bryer made the perfectly valid and well-argued point:

'For God's sake! You're in New York, where nobody gives a shit.'

Now, since that sage advice from the GLW, some say FPO (Fun Prevention Officer), since then, I have gathered about the place a decent number of summer hats, and a couple of winter jobs.

This hat thing, it's not a question of affectation, or of a vanity driven thing as cover for lack of thatch on my upper reaches (well, not *much*). It's really more of a practical consideration. In summer it keeps the heat out, and in winter it seals it in. Believe me, a strawberry tint which gives the skin drawn over the skull bone the aspect of a crimson light-bulb is not a winning look. Being caught in a hailstorm, hatless and at my time of recede is also no laughing matter. Unless, of course, you happen to be an onlooker.

So, this is no Hollies' drummer disguise. Seriously, Hollies sticksman Bobby Elliot has rarely been seen giving his top deck an airing since about 1965. Look him up in the Google pages, lot of hats.

Some years ago, American friends gifted me membership of the honourable order of Kentucky Colonels. So that's me, and among others, Bob Hope, Elvis, Ann Margret, and Muhammad Ali. There may be a Pope or two in there too. There usually is. Invitation only. Although the honour doesn't give me automatic access to the golden circle at The Kentucky *Derby* and all of the food and beverage that might entail, I do have a humungous great framed certificate on which my name is picked out in finest copperplate and surrounded by official wax seals, flashy endorsing signatures and suitable blue and gold be-ribbonment. But best of all, I was also given one of those *tall* baseball caps. A real Good 'ol Boy Southern cracker style one, the kind where the front bit rises up so it's as long as your face. Also, when this hat was commissioned it must have come as a great relief to all those employed in the gold braid industry, and plainly there are many.

My Kentucky Colonels baseball cap is an awesome thing. The only trouble is that I am on a second yellow card with the FPO, so if I ever wear it again it's us for the quickie divorce and she'll be away with Johnny Depp or Rod Stewart, and I'll have to give Uma Thurman another try. Nightmare that woman, honestly.

Had the black fedora on the other morning, walked into the railway station ticket office and the lovely Jan said:

'Wow, you look so dashing in that hat.'

"Thanks Jan," I replied, glancing up shyly from under the brim like a Jane Austen heroine.

'Yes,' she said, 'I didn't recognise you.'

Now, coming home on the train the other night, had to meet someone for a beer, so I'm late-ish. Late-ish into my local station which is in an area you might describe as *lively,* an area where someone who might usually be sporting a waistcoat, a long, flowing scarf draped round their neck, topped off with an attention-grabbing hat might as well ditch that lot and replace them with a sign round their neck which says 'Feel free to kick me and relieve me of my valuables of which I have many'.

Still, if I were to wear it all the time it wouldn't be fun, now would it?

Snapper

'*D*id you bring the camera?' asks Sandra.

Because with a day at the beach or the zoo ahead and small child in tow, why wouldn't you make sure you remembered to bring the camera? Because we're not very good at taking photos, that's why.

On holiday, we'll see some interesting sight, and one of us will say, 'You going to take a picture?' and the other will reply, 'No, you do it', and this interchangeable conversation will continue like this for the duration. So much so that we'll invariably panic on the last day and take a load of pictures which means that in our holiday snaps there's often a large batch where we're wearing the same clothes.

'Go and stand over there,' one will say.
'No, you go, I'll take it'.

For there's only one thing worse than taking the picture and that's being in it. Just last week at a very famous historical building in a place which attracts a vast number of tourists each year, I saw a lone young woman set up her tripod and camera, fiddle with the timer and go and stand in the front of this landmark with a stupid smile on her face. On her own. I am far too self-conscious to do such a thing alone. When Sandra has camera poised I might say, "I'll do it, just be quick," and I'll stand, generally stony faced and uncomfortable until the ordeal is over. In this way, many scenes of great beauty have been ruined by my miserable countenance.

So perhaps Sandra and I weren't suited to an African safari? On the flight out to Kenya, after take-off, the man across the aisle rummaged in his carry-on bag, pulled out, I'd guess a high several hundred quid's worth, of brand new, still in the box, professional-style, photographic recording device. A multitude of lenses, varying in size from extra-large to bleedin' humungous, dials and straps, and matt black and silver trim all over the shop. He waved away the drinks trolley, slung the camera round his neck, propped the Lord of the Rings sized manual on his tray table and for the rest of the flight he learned how to use his camera. Us? Well, now we were feeling that our 10-year-old Minolta might not be up to the job ahead, but at least we each had a drink.

Ah, Kenya. Where, in the Tsavo game park, we saw lots of exotic animals, many of which we'd only seen before on the TV, slit from arse to tit and with a blood-bearded lion poking around their insides. After a day or so, the guide will point and say, 'zebra' or 'warthog' or 'antelope', and we'd find ourselves coming over all Roman Emperor, mentally waving him away, and thinking, 'Zebras bore me, show me something else'. Cheetahs. All credit to the bloke, he found us some cheetahs. Which were a bit elusive, but we tracked them, well chased them really, and as we did so, many of our number were clicking away. I took a few, not many, because I wanted to see these animals with my own eyes, not through a lens. You know, true memory beats all, pictures better on the radio. All that nonsense.

London. Six films to have developed, yes, it really was that long ago. Six films, not many cheetahs. I called in to pick them up. 'Forty pounds please, said the bloke. "What? That can't be right," I replied. He insisted. I demanded to see the manager, who confirmed the charge was indeed forty quid. I divvied up with 2 twenties, and a parting shot. "You're a robber," I said. That's told him. 'What?' he replied. "You're a robber," I repeated, and that told him again.

I relayed the conversation to Sandra when I got home. '40 quid?' She said, 'sounds about right'. Thank God for digital, eh?

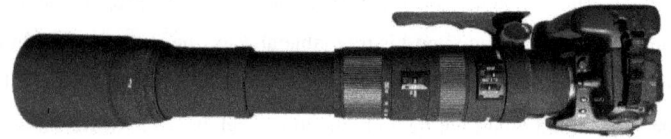

Bob

*B*ob Dylan at The Royal Albert Hall

"Never seen him before," I said to friends and random strangers, who, without exception replied by saying, 'I saw him at Blackbushe, you know with Eric Clapton?' Everyone I speak to about anything was at that concert, except me. I don't know why, perhaps like The Who at Charlton, it was another iconic show that I missed because I couldn't raise the 2 quid ticket price.

I had been insanely excited for months, and as show-time approached I found myself on what I assume is The Dark Internet I'd heard so much about, where nothing is discussed but Bob and what he played last night. Not everyone's a fan, of course. A mate of mine speaks up for Neil Young over Dylan – personally, like The Beatles/Stones thing, I see no need to choose, and anyway, all right-thinking people know it's The Beatles and Dylan all day long, right? My friend in the Neil Young camp believes that the Dylan canon would be improved beyond measure if the vocals were removed from every song. I know, I know, a Neil Young fan getting fussy about vocal stylings, you couldn't make it up. It's a bit like Hitler calling Pol Pot's methods into question.

One morning I was reading an online review in The Blackpool Gazette of the previous night's show at The Winter Gardens. 'Who's that,' asked Sandra as she glimpsed the picture of the grizzled old geezer crouching underneath what appeared to be one of Phil Spector's old syrups. "Bob Dylan," says I. 'JEESUS! *Really*?!' she replied.

As she said the week before, 'I'm looking forward to it. I mean, I'm not his biggest fan, but I think he's very clever'. Which is fair enough, considering what I've put her through.

I mean, there was a 5-star review in The Times of a preceding show in Glasgow. I said, you know, it's worth reading this, and left it lying around in all sorts of accessible locations, so that she might read the bit that explains he's not singing off key and struggling to hit the notes, he's using his voice as a musical instrument, see? Might have saved all sorts of trouble on a Thursday night in Kensington. Had she glanced at it? Not a peep. Me? Read it 6 times at least, and then went back a few times to check that I hadn't missed anything.

Long time ago, I decided Sandra didn't much care for Dylan because she hadn't, you know, heard the records properly so I set out to play her a few so that we could enjoy them together and I could answer any questions she might have. I know, what a wanker. So, that night I played her more Dylan than an agnostic could reasonably be expected to bear, and to her great credit she bore this ordeal of Biblical proportions with great fortitude, love and forbearance.

Right up until she said, 'I agree, he's brilliant, a genius. Now can we have the TV back on?'

Heaven

I can't deny that I laugh up my sleeve at descriptions of the facilities enjoyed by modern festival-goers. A VIP area that's available to those who are prepared to pay extra. Including VIP toilets. All sorts of food stalls: pies containing actual meat and proper curries and Chinese and vegetarian stalls who sell peanut butter you could artex a ceiling with – you'd certainly be ill-advised to introduce it into your digestive system. I suppose you might compress it into missiles to chuck at a deserving artiste – The Red Hot Chilli Peppers, perhaps. Or whoever's being James Blunt this year.

I hear tell of jugglers and clowns and all sorts of different stages and tents. All in the name of entertainment. Well, not in my day. If some addle-headed promoter had seen fit to try pitching a comedy tent at Reading Festival in its darkest days the likely outcome would have been a thousand people gaining swift possession of tattered canvas flags which would soon be daubed with encouraging slogans like: *John Peel's a See-You-Next-Tuesday*, and the festival site would be bordered by poles bearing the bloodied heads of comedians.

Because, let me tell you, concert-going in those days was no laughing matter. To take you indoors for a moment, I went to see Camel performing their epic take on *The Snow Goose* at Reading Town Hall on a bitter January night, a night when the janitor clearly thought that having any form of heating on might release the stink of five-hundred hippies into his auditorium and that wasn't a risk he was prepared to take. It's not as if I cared much for Camel and their rather dreary *Snow Goose*, more that I was keen on Maria who was keen on Camel and I thought that by showing an interest…. Deluded teenage boys, eh? It was far too cold for any of that nonsense.

Often going to a concert involved the seeking out of small comforts. A heater at Reading bus station, We also tried to get warm by huddling around a cigarette lighter. A dry patch of grass at a festival, an ice cream van that sold something other than disgusting Players No.10 fags, scoring some food that was free of botulism, not getting beaten up at a Milton Keynes mudbath-cum-bloodbath, or perhaps a comfortable seat.

A Thin Lizzy concert at a small venue. We stood close to the stage, and to one side, just behind a row of cables and some gear, there was a single, wooden chair. One of our group, Matt, stepped over this obstruction and, while giving a cheery wave in our direction, sat down and made himself comfortable. The smug look on his face remained in place right up until the moment one of Lizzy's road crew appeared and enquired politely as to what the goodness he thought he was doing. I wonder if Matt ever managed to extricate himself from head-first bass bin insertion?

So, at indoor events, you can't smoke or drink, and if you don't choose your seat carefully at a large venue you might well end up with vertigo, and everything smells of chips.

But outdoors, it's fun and luxury all the way, I hear. All farmers market and street fair with added Kasabian. So perhaps not all good. Whereas back then, we festival goers were corralled into an enclosure and pretty much left to our own devices.

Woodstock MC, Wavy Gravy famously pronounced from the stage:

We must be in heaven man!

Do me favour Wavy, and shut your neck. Those most definitely are not the sentiments of the bloke half-a-mile back who's got someone sitting on his feet.

Safe

*W*ith Ladder Awareness Week nearly upon as again, well, as far as I know Ladder Awareness Week may still be some way off, but hey-ho. Safety in general around the household and what can go wrong, eh? Now there's a subject. Hopefully.

Mrs Bryer tells me the story of when her father was high up on the home scaffolding unit, in the act of applying well-loaded paintbrush to wall, when the scaffolding unit, the *wheeled* scaffolding unit decided to make things interesting by going for a bit of an unplanned roll. Now, whether this resulted in the wall bearing the image of a freshly-painted arch tailing off into the distance is not recorded, but it's an arresting image, right?

Sandra put her own take on her dad's stunt-decorating by not applying enough wallpaper-paste, and then not being able to reach *quite* high enough and thus ended up being draped from nut to knees in a good length of cascading wallpaper, and then falling off the ladder.

My old man, worked for a spell as an electrician on an army camp. Where one day his duties required him to go round all of the street lights on the army housing estate, and check them out, re-lamping as necessary. Up the ladder to the top, down the ladder, up the ladder *et cetera et cetera*. Add in the fact it was the school holidays and he had to guard against the van being robbed at every turn by gobby little horrors and you can imagine the sort of day he was having. So it's perhaps understandable that his concentration wavered, he got tired, I expect, but whatever the reason, at one stage of the afternoon he slipped and the ladder peeled away from beneath him. Luckily he managed to cling onto the top of the post and swung there in the breeze. No doubt with a cigar clamped between his teeth. Still, help would surely be on the way soon enough, right? Well, not necessarily. This bunch of army brats, army brats being as army brats does, were less interested in playing the Good Samaritans than they were in taking bets as to *when* exactly he would fall, and how many, if any, limbs would survive intact.

Our youngest son moved into a new house recently, and being very keen and rather good at all of this DIY stuff, he had the floorboards up in the rather chilly master bedroom in no time so he could install extra insulation. Now, the master bedroom was situated above the garage, and one sunny morning it seems he thought, 'Well, I *could* go down the stairs and out of the back door and through to the garage but maybe there's a quicker waaaaay..' And indeed there was. The fast way. Straight through the ceiling. I tried to help by suggesting he install a firemans' pole *and* I bought him a *Spiderman* comic, but can you believe my gestures were construed as being insensitive?

Me. Me who only the other week, in the teeth of a midnight hurricane exited the marital bed and set out to move a 6-foot fence panel which had blown its moorings to a place of safety. In the course of this mercy mission me and the panel were suddenly snatched up by a severe gust. The panel went one way, and I was slammed head-first into the turf some 20 feet away missing the concrete bird bath by the width of the skin on a gnat's cock.

Not my forte, really, manual stuff. As illustrated by a forever puzzling moment. I went up for a bath after a day's decorating, only to find I'd somehow managed to embellish my testicles with gloss paint.

Hobby

*P*eople like to collect stuff don't they? Be it objects of tangible worth and aesthetic appeal, or the Green Shield Stamps that my parents used get from the petrol station and stick in little books. Trading them in later for a set of table mats featuring scenes from the hunt or maybe an attractive carriage clock as a feature for the mantelpiece. They also had heaps of bright blue Embassy fag coupons sorted into elastically banded bundles of, I don't know, a thousand points each, all in a shoebox under the stairs, and when we had enough, we'd send off for whatever they had in *their* catalogue. Remembering the rate at which the old man went through the Embassy Filters, I'd guess we sent the coupons off quite often.

Me? Well, at that time I collected football stickers and Esso World Cup Coins. Had the lot too, mounted in the official Esso World Cup mounty thing. Binned long ago, and probably worth thousands now. I remember slinging a load of old magazines into a skip at the recycling depot, I mention this because I see that issue 1 of *Mojo* magazine, which, as it had John Lennon and Bob Dylan on the cover, I bought on publication and possibly before the ink had dried. Anyway, bought it, read it, kept it a long time until it fell victim to a cull, and I see that a vintage magazine website is offering the self-same copy this very week for eighty-five of your English Pounds.

I don't mind a bit of *Bargain Hunt* on a lunchtime if I'm at home. You know, people go to antique fairs and buy stuff and try to sell it at auction for a profit – which is surely the wrong way round financially, if not in terms of dramatic tension. But when I see people buying a few vintage spoons in a case or an ornamental fork, I can't help wondering what on earth they do with them. Get them out every now and again and look at them, I suppose.

Or worse, they get them out when they have friends round – 'Would you like to look at my spoons?' Rather like those people who used to put their holiday snaps on slides and show them to you, 'Ready? Everyone got a drink? OK. Pop the lights off would you Marjorie?' Sorry, I appear to have strayed into Seventies' BBC sitcom-land. Back to the res.

Unfortunately, they like to share. My nephew, Will O'Donnell, creative genius of The Dirty Truth. Who they? The best band you haven't heard yet, that's who. Will tells of a time when he flirted with taking the corporate shilling, and right from the off his new boss was so keen to share his hobby with him, that he brought in photos detailing his progress in putting together a replica of The Cutty Sark using just matchsticks, glue and a lonely existence.

An occasional drinking pal, Martin, inspired this piece when he told me about going into a pub and being buttonholed by someone he'd never met before who asked him right out, 'Do you like ferrets?' 'Not really,' Martin replied, not unreasonably. But the stranger persisted, 'Know anything about 'em?' 'No,' was Martin's firm reply. Well, as Martin tells it, the ferret man proceeded to fill him in on every detail he might possibly need were he to perform a U-turn and take up ferreting and ferrety things in all their stinking glory. The genius of this tactic of course, is that Martin can no longer feign ignorance. He's been briefed, and nowadays the ferret man greets him as a fellow-furry fancier and feels free to forge forth fully unflustered on all things ferret.

Formality

I found a letter on the train the other day. It was addressed to a university professor and it seemed important, so I looked him up, emailed him and sent it on. My initial email began, *Dear Professor*, he answered me with *Dear Mr Bryer*, but after just a couple of exchanges we were plain old *Steve* and *Phil* to each other. But that's OK, because we'd been through the formalities.

There's a swanky hotel near where I work, where I've been known to pause for the occasional pint while using it as an impromptu railway waiting room. This is a place where the bow-tied barman in his crisp white shirt is all full of *Yes Sirs* and *Thank you Madams*. Except it seems when I bowl up to the bar and am addressed with a cheery *Yes Mate?*

I was disconcerted the other evening to be fawned over by the barman in a local pub-come-eaterie with his unnecessarily over-the-top enquiries of, 'How is the sausage and mash, sir?' However, I felt I was due a wee bit more respect from the barman in the posh place. Especially considering what they charge for a pint of Old Speckled Hen.

What can I get you guys?
No worries.
No worries *at all*.
I'm good, thanks.
Are you good?
It's all good then?

No it bloody isn't. All of these are things that I don't wish to hear in restaurants. Alright pal? There's some footage of a callow American promoter addressed fearsome Led Zeppelin manager Peter Grant as *Pal*. Cue full storm force warning as Grant slips into murderous rage. 'Pal? *Pal? How dare you? I'm not your pal, we haven't even been introduced*'. Undoubtedly a formidable adversary and, should you get on the wrong side him, apparently a rather nasty piece of work, however, here he makes a valid point. He may have done it while jabbing someone in the chest with his big, fat fingers but I'm guessing that once word got round few were dumb enough to be quite so familiar.

A letter arrives from a well-known airline. OK, it was Virgin Atlantic. Not a circular or anything like that, it's a letter confirming a booking. *Hi there*, it begins. Hi there? How about a bit of *Dear Mr Bryer* when there'll be a four-figure sum heading your way? I'm due a touch of *Dear Sir*, surely? And not as someone else once wrote to me at work, *Dear Valued Customer*.

I don't mind being called mate, as long it suits the circumstances, and in Australia I don't mind being called mate whatever the circumstances. Because out there, with their open, informal, cheery manner, everyone's your mate and everyone will call you mate. Even the ones who think you're a pommy bastard.

I'll wish you Best Regards before I go, or as some wind up their emails, BR. How insulting is that? You're only worth 2 letters, which rather detracts from the supposed sentiments of the sign-off, doesn't it? And by the way, if I'm so important to you…

Yours sincerely...

Writing a book isn't the half of it. Finish a book and you haven't even started. You've got to get out there and promote it. Which, when I wrote my first novel, *None of your Business,* is what I tried to do.

To my surprise, and no doubt that of the listener, I blagged an interview slot on the local BBC radio station, managed to secure a bit of local press coverage, and made a nuisance of myself by engaging in some quiet self-promotion on a variety of internet forums. One of which brooked no such nonsense from the likes of me and were swift and merciless in imposing a lifetime ban.

In the naïve hope of securing a review slot in a national paper or magazine I sent out multiple copies to editors. Still, no hard feelings, we've all come to embrace recycling haven't we? And anyway, a couple of American websites, proper business ones, embraced the concept and were good enough to print a few kind words of review and recommendation, and, joy of all joys, a click-to-buy link to everyone's favourite online bookstore.

Some telly and film people had nice things to say. A film producer and a noted literary agent were generous with their time and advice. Clearly I should press on and take every opportunity to promote the book. A stall at the village fete offering signed copies? Why not?

Here's why not.

To the side of the arena where later the majorettes would march and the dogs be shown, we set up a garden table with a tablecloth draped over it, a poster which Sandra had put together on Photoshop bore a précis of the novel, *None of your Business*, and a big picture of the author. The poster was fixed to card and propped up on Sandra's easel. Front of house and visible we had a bowl of apples, a bowl of sweets, a pile of books, my lovely assistant Sandra, me, and a biro. Under the table was an ashtray, cigarettes, lighter, and a coolbox filled with dry white wine and cans of Guinness.

It had been drizzling, so the garden parasol was up and we had our coats on. We were next to the ice cream van so spent the day engulfed in the aroma of sugary diesel. People strode past, keeping their distance, it seemed. "Don't scowl at people," I said to Sandra. "Give 'em a smile." Although I had to agree that it was becoming hard to keep the spirits up. Someone came over and asked what the book was about. I gave her an outline. 'How much is it?' Well, my answer slammed the door on that prospective deal. I hadn't appreciated that this was the sort of event to which people brought a pocketful of change and were as likely to part with a tenner as they were to turn out to be Steven Spielberg in disguise. I sold one copy all day, and that was to the bloke who ran the fete. I suppose as it had cost a fiver to rent the space that I came out ahead. Although as people became less timid they descended like starlings on the free apples and sweets, so maybe I broke even.

The breakfast DJ from the local commercial station came over. 'Have to get you on the show one morning,' he said. Things were looking up, but then, oh dear, oh dear. With pen poised over his buckshee copy, I paused and said, "Sorry, what was your name again?" 'Dave,' he replied stiffly. Although he may just as well have said, 'Invitation withdrawn'.

Birds

*E*ver been on one of those trips the holiday rep tries to push on you? On a minibus and thrown into the company of a bunch of people who under normal circumstances you'd have nothing whatever to do with, or perhaps with whom to do? We did once.

This looks alright, we said, *Nature trail, including lunch*. Be nice to see a bit of the island, wouldn't it? Because after 3 days of tucking into the goodies on offer on our first all-inclusive holiday we realised that me drinking beer for 2 weeks was ultimately no sort of break. Anyway, I was over it by now. "I went up to the bar and asked for a beer and he just gave me one, no money, nothing to sign. I'm going to drink this one and then go up and see if he does it again". That pretty much sums up the first few days on Tobago.

So, we sign up for a day immersed in the delights of the local flora and fauna and, in all probability a delicious seafood lunch swilled down with plenty of cold beer – which we would doubtless need after the morning's gentle stroll about the woods.

The guide picked us up at 8AM. A tidy little chap with a silver beard who wouldn't have looked out of place in the *Hobbit* films, if it wasn't for the fact he was kitted out in matching khaki safari shirt and shorts. He was quick to inform us that he showed David Attenborough around when he visited with a BBC crew to film some bird or other.

We were first pick-up, and as we called at a few more hotels and our party swelled to an even dozen, all of whom had been swiftly made aware of the Attenborough connection, we noticed something rather troubling. While

Sandra had a small handbag containing water, cigarettes and emergency lipstick, and I carried more fags and a back-up lighter, our travelling companions were well-kitted out with all manner of gear, and all of them without exception carried binoculars and neat little notebooks.

At the first point of call, when we had to creep through a wood as quietly as possible because some scruffy little sparrow-like thing was flitting about in the dust and everyone was incomprehensibly excited to see it, well, it became apparent that we had dropped an enormous brick by booking ourselves on the serious birdwatchers tour. Twitchers for the day, and it was soon obvious to all present that we didn't belong. I'm afraid we regressed to *teenagerdom* and took to mucking about at the back of the virtual classroom, for that is what it felt like. Our guide spotted something and went into a hunter's crouch, he crept forwards and waved his hand in a beckoning motion at those in his wake who he hadn't seen yet. By some miscalculation we had wandered forwards and would have been caught up in some serious twitching, were it not for the fact that as soon as our guide glanced back to see who was with him and saw it was us he shook his head in disappointment and gave up the chase.

To lunch at last. Beer and lobster. Get in. 'Fruit juice sir?' "No thanks, beer please". 'Sorry sir we only serve soft drinks at Maisie's Vegetarian Restaurant'. Now, I've nothing against veggie food, I've nothing against soft drinks, but as the disappointments of the morning had mounted, thoughts of lunch were about all I had left to cling onto. We considered bailing out there and then, but as we were on the wrong side of the island and in a rainforest which lacked both bus-stop and taxi rank we were rather stuck with it.

We all boarded a little boat which would take us to the island of Little Tobago where a load more bloody birds lived up a bloody great hill which is a bugger to climb up in 40 degrees of heat while stony sober. Still we got up there where there was no shade and we had to keep really still and quiet as these bleedin' birds flew about until they landed and took off again and flew about and landed and took off and landed... 'David Attenborough's been up here you know...'

Musical

*Y*es, I was that soldier. I sat in the Cambridge Theatre in the heart of London's glittering West End at the extra matinee showing of the musical adaptation of the great Roald Dahl's story *Matilda*. The key phrase that I just said there, did you hear it? The key phrase was 'musical'. For, having let out a deep and resigned sigh as I cast my gaze around the place at 14:25, or as we theatrical experts might put it, 5 minutes before the horror begins, I started to think this might have not been the A1, 5-star number one, double-first plan after all.

Five-minutes into the first song, I leant chin on upturned palm, sucked on a consolation polo mint and watched the drama unfold. As an excited, excitable, ultimately perhaps *executionable* cast of adorable little cherubic stage school brats sang their little heads off and achieved comparable volume to that of the Saturn V rocket on take-off to the Moon but at the musical pitch known as *screech*, I pushed an index finger into each ear and remembered all of a sudden why I don't much care for musicals.

Still, only 2 hours and 40 minutes to go. Before the off, I checked with the young lady in the bar about interval time. I'm hoping for 40 minutes. 15, she said. 15! Hardly worth getting out of your seat, I thought. A thought I was to revise rather swiftly after... well, who knows how long of rather irritating tunes belted out by a cast who were becoming less adorable by each and every hideous verse. Particularly those who played the older children. There may still be an audience for strapping young men in long grey socks, shorts and fifth-form issue V-neck jumpers, but personally I'd hoped it had died out with Hitler.

When I sloped out for a slash, I even overcame my *Oh, I do despair, I really do* interval disappointment at the choice of beer. *'Becks or Stella?'*.

"Um, Becks, please." £4.50 a bottle, and, because, unless it's the last of the brandy, I detest drinking out of bottles, this thin, ordinary and warmish brew is served in an enormous plastic pot more suited to housing an aspidistra, and I've got 5 minutes in which to drink it. You know what? I'd have paid double.

I had a chat to someone at work about the musical theatre experience. She said she struggled when she saw *Annie*. You know, *the sun'll come out tomorrow* one. Never seen it but can well believe it. Then she recommended *Phantom of the Opera*. She was plainly very keen on it and I didn't want to be rude, so I just said, that, well, I wasn't really a fan of the music. 'Now, *We Will Rock You* is great,' she said, 'You know the Queen one?' Bloody hell, people don't make it easy do they? Again, I said, I just don't like Queen. 'My friend doesn't like Queen either,' she said, 'But she loved it'. Well OK. 'Ben Elton's script is really quite funny,' she continued. I may have said something like I'm not buying it.

'But the atmosphere in theatre is brilliant,' she said.

A roomful of Queen fans up for a party? Now you've convinced me.

I'm the one on the right:

Film

"Shall we watch a film tonight?"

So it begins, the latest instalment in the Saturday horror show which is going through the Sky Movies On Demand A-Z.

Obviously we have to have the unanimous agreement of the pair of us for a movie to pass muster. Or at least a 75% approval rating, where one says, 'Would you like to see this one?' and the other replies, 'I don't mind.' Which means, if I'm the waverer, that I'll have picked up a book after 20 minutes anyway, or if it's Sandra then her 'I don't mind' means she'll have gone to bed to a similar timescale.

To save time, there are certain code-words which mean the film in question never gets to the discussion stage:

Touching family drama
Madcap family fun
Family fun adventure
Feelgood family drama
Singleton
Sparky rom-com
Sassy comedy
Cute canine caper
Foxy crimefighters
Uplifting
Sweet romance
Free spirit
Troubled relationship
Fangtastic comedy horror

Frothy
Grieving couple
Terminally ill
Tear-jerker
Quirky comedy
Quirky drama
Quirky horror

Rom-com generally gets yellow card from me, and we saw something last week described a dramedy. There's bromantic comedy too of course, so I'm sure a romdram can't be far away, if it's not already among us baring its terrible teeth. They should bear in mind though, the risk of confusing stupid people. Someone of my acquaintance asked on more than one occasion, "What's bio*pic*? Says here Johnny Cash Biopic. Is he ill or something? Like bipolar or dyslexic?"

Further shorthand for killing a film stony dead involves us invoking one of the following phrases:

Two words – Richard Curtis, or
Two words – Adam Sandler, or
Two words – Owen Wilson.

You get the idea.

One word – *Matilda*. Still not over the musical experience, you see, so anything associated gets the flick as matter of course.

Three words – Sarah Jessica and Parker.

The possibilities are boundless.

School stuff generally gets not much shrift:

Coming of age drama
High school
Dysfunctional school
Troubled youngster
Slam-dunkin' drama

Of course, the ones to make you claw your eyes out and stuff them into your ears so you might completely avoid anything described with the words:

Little league baseball, or:
From the director *Saw 2, 3* and *4*.

I see that nowadays 'heartwarming and heartrending have been slimmed down simply to 'warming'. Which surely doesn't mean what's intended. A bit like *Bad Boys 2*, which is described in the programme guide as 'bombastic action'. Definition of bombastic? : *inflated, pretentious, pompous and overblown.* So, even though I haven't seen any of the *Bad Boys* series, I'm guessing that sometimes Sky get it right.

A film called *Battleship* has the handy warning that it contains violence, flashing images and Rihanna.

One starring 2-bob shouty bloke, 50 Cent is tagged as, ahem, ' A raps to riches drama'. Which should surely be enough to get the originator fired and their fingers broken.

However, however obvious, I do like this description, 'Sweaty welder by day, sexy stripper by night'. If only because I feel they might be interchangeable.

Read this one last week, 'Terminally ill teenager with Dakota Fanning'. Which I assumed was the name of a new disease. 'Got a nasty touch of Dakota Fanning, haven't I?'

And as I have to be really keen on something to devote more than a couple of hours to it, anything over 120 minutes is often arbitrarily ruled out which narrows the field even further. Is it any wonder we often end up saying, "So, we'll watch the Cary Grant one, yeah?"

Hang on though, in the interests of research I've been going through the guide again. Here's one:

"By night she's a music hall star, but by day she's New York's premier crime-fighter".

"Mmm, sounds alright. What's it called?"

"Tarara Boom D.A."*

---

*The provenance is a little murky, but I believe I have Frank Muir and Denis Norden to thank for this joke. Also Danny Baker for pointing it out.

www.ingramcontent.com/pod-product-compliance
Lightning Source LLC
Chambersburg PA
CBHW061440040426
42450CB00007B/1136